POCKET GUIDE

BIRDS
OF SOUTHERN AFRICA

IAN SINCLAIR

Dedicated to Daryn and Kiera

Published by Struik Nature
(an imprint of Penguin Random House (Pty) Ltd)
Reg. No. 1953/000441/07
The Estuaries, No. 4, Oxbow Crescent, Century Avenue, Century City 7441
PO Box 1144, Cape Town, 8000 South Africa

Visit **www.randomstruik.co.za** and join the Struik Nature Club
for updates, news, events and special offers.

First published in 2009

9 10 8

Publisher: Pippa Parker
Managing editor: Helen de Villiers
Editor: Joy Clack
Project manager: Colette Alves
Proofreader: Emsie du Plessis
Design director: Janice Evans
Designer: Louise Topping

Reproduction by Hirt & Carter Cape (Pty) Ltd
Printed and bound by RR Donnelley Asia Printing Solutions Ltd

ISBN 978 1 77007 769 0
(ePUB) 978 1 77584 468 6
(ePDF) 978 1 77584 469 3

Also available in Afrikaans as *Sakgids: Voëls van Suider-Afrika*
ISBN 978 1 77007 770 6

MIX
Paper from
responsible sources
FSC® C101537
www.fsc.org

Page 1: Little Bee-eater; Page 3: Namaqua Dove (top left), Orange-breasted Sunbird
(top right), Malachite Kingfisher (bottom left), Village Weaver (bottom right)

CONTENTS

Introduction	4
Bird habitats in southern Africa	6
How to use this book	8
Glossary	10
Species accounts	12
Further reading	138
Photographic credits	138
Index	140

INTRODUCTION

Southern Africa is prime birdwatching terrain, supporting as it does almost 1 000 bird species, which is about 10 per cent of the world's entire bird population. Some 170 of these, particularly in the southwestern regions, are endemics (meaning they are found nowhere else in the world); the more tropical north and east of the region are known for their astonishing diversity of birds; and the coastal regions offer a variety of pelagic birds.

This handy-format, compact guide will help birders identify most of the many birds encountered on day trips and longer birding holidays. With the advent of digital photography a whole new range of excellent images has become available. This pocket guide features photographic identification of 500 birds, and includes species from South Africa, Namibia, Botswana, Zimbabwe and Mozambique. It gives identification details and where they differ, describes females, juveniles and immatures. Specific flight patterns are discussed where this facilitates identification. It also offers details of habitat, status, call and bird size.

Collared Sunbird

The featured species are not necessarily the most common in southern Africa, but they are usually the more conspicuous birds and are thus more likely to be encountered – along the coasts, in nature or game reserves, and even in urban areas.

Although most birds are visible, and many are abundant, they are not always easy to identify correctly. If a bird is not clearly seen, or is seen for only a short period, or if a feature on the bird appears exaggerated, it could lead to misidentification. We are more likely to make the correct identification by aiming for sustained and better viewing of these elusive creatures. Readers are encouraged to familiarise themselves with the different species by leafing through the book in order to recognise a range of birds before

African Fish-Eagle

even encountering them. When confronted with a bird that's hard to identify, first judge its size, then try to work out its general shape, colour pattern, the length of its tail, shape of its wings and any other detail that might be conspicuous. Often there is one striking feature that is sufficient to distinguish the bird, but sometimes it takes the combination of several features to make a positive identification. By using this book in the field you should be able to identify the birds you have seen, or at least be able to narrow down the search to particular bird families and then later identify them at home using one of the more comprehensive birding books.

Cape Gannet

In theory, the most satisfactory way to be certain of an identification is to photograph the bird and then, at your leisure, identify it from the photograph by consulting books or by showing the photograph to an expert. This is now quite feasible, using a digital camera with 10x zoom – even one of the less expensive models available today. An alternative

Crested Guineafowl

idea is to use a notebook and pencil to jot down details of the bird you are watching and to make a rudimentary sketch showing its obvious features. From your notes and sketches the bird should be relatively easy to identify at a later stage.

Seasoned birders will have acquired various pieces of equipment to help in their birding ventures; help is available in books and on the Internet about which binoculars, telescope, tape recorder/iPod, etc, will best suit your purposes, as well as advice on where and when to go birding in southern Africa. Courses on bird identification are offered by clubs, societies and universities, and these all help to hone your skills in the field. There is, however, no substitute for first-hand observation: the longer you spend in the field improving your ability to identify birds correctly, the greater will be your understanding of – and pleasure in – birding in general.

BIRD HABITATS OF SOUTHERN AFRICA

The map of the region (right) shows the major vegetation zones (biomes) mentioned in the text. Bird distribution may be contained by, or even restricted to, specialised habitats within these zones; some birds, however, may be widespread and occur across several vegetation zones.

Namib Desert

This biome is characterised by stony plains, sand dunes and rocky hills and mountains. It is an area of low rainfall and is sparsely vegetated.

Fynbos

The fynbos biome is confined to the southern and western extremes of South Africa and enjoys a Mediterranean climate with wet winters and hot, windy summers. The vegetation is shrubby and comprises a rich variety of proteas, ericas and restios.

Forests

The forest biome occurs in scattered patches on the eastern and northeastern parts of the subregion. It is divided into afromontane (or montane) forest, found at higher altitudes, and lowland forest, confined to low altitudes.

Savanna

This habitat, also known as 'bushveld', is characterised by wooded grasslands. Arid savanna (thornveld) characterises vegetation in the western part of the subregion and is dominated by *Acacia* species; moist savanna in the northern and eastern parts enjoys higher rainfall.

Karoo

The two Karoo biomes occur in the arid southwestern part of the subregion. Succulent Karoo occurs in winter-rainfall areas, while Nama Karoo is in summer-rainfall areas. Both biomes are semi-desert shrublands with stony plains scattered with small plants.

Grassland

The grassland biome occurs at a variety of altitudes. It is a high-rainfall habitat, dominated by grasses, with woody plants being either rare or absent.

VEGETATION MAP OF SOUTHERN AFRICA

- Namib Desert
- Fynbos
- Lowland forest
- Afromontane forest
- Moist savanna
- Arid savanna
- Karoo
- Grassland

The Cape Sugarbird inhabits the fynbos biome.

HOW TO USE THIS BOOK

This pocket-sized book has been designed primarily for use in the field, but you can reap further benefits by paging through it at your leisure. If you look at the photographs frequently, you will come to recognise a fair selection of the featured birds when you encounter them in the field, with the exception of the more unremarkable or nondescript species.

Features of the book:

1 Photograph shows male in breeding plumage unless otherwise indicated. Insets show female or immature birds where they differ, or may show non-breeding male where relevant.

2 Distribution map shows where the species is found in southern Africa. Solid colour reflects where the bird is most common; tinted colour indicates where it is scarcer.

3 Text highlights characteristics that will aid identification, including appearance, habitat and call. The species' status gives an indication of its relative abundance within the region: common, vulnerable, endangered, etc.

4 Size for all species, except the ostrich (where the height is given), is the length from bill tip to tip of the outstretched tail. Where the male is larger than the female, two size ranges are given.

5 Where the breeding male develops a longer tail, the tail length is mentioned separately in the text.

6 Seasonality bar indicates, at a glance, when the bird is present in the region. The darker shade reflects months in which the bird is more visible/abundant. White indicates absence from the region.

7 Breeding season: the months in which the bird breeds and in some species is thus more colourful and conspicuous. The months stated are an aggregate of all breeding months and locations across the region.

8 NE/E/BrE shows at a glance if a bird is near endemic, endemic or a breeding endemic.

Abbreviations used in this book

ad. = **adult**
imm. = **immature**
br. = **breeding**
non-br. = **non-breeding**
E = **endemic**

BrE = **breeding endemic**
NE = **near endemic**
♀ = **female**
♂ = **male**

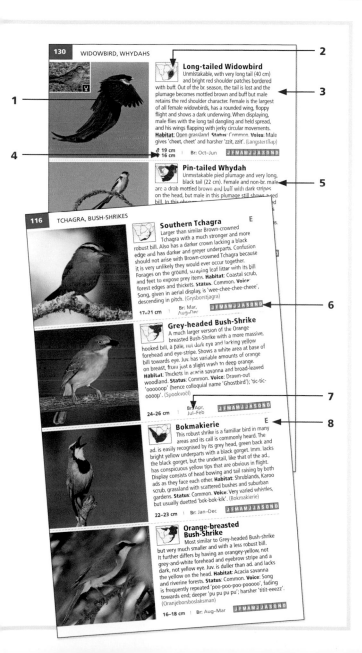

Long-tailed Widowbird

Unmistakable, with very long tail (40 cm) and bright red shoulder patches bordered with buff. Out of the br. season, the tail is lost and the plumage becomes mottled brown and buff but male retains the red shoulder character. Female is the largest of all female widowbirds, has a rounded wing, floppy flight and shows a dark underwing. When displaying, male flies with the long tail dangling and held spread, and his wings flapping with jerky circular movements. **Habitat**: Open grassland **Status**: Common. **Voice**: Male gives 'cheet, cheet' and harsher 'zzit, zzit'. (Langstertflap)

♂ 19 cm
♀ 16 cm | Br: Oct–Jun J F M A M J J A S O N D

Pin-tailed Whydah

Unmistakable pied plumage and very long, black tail (22 cm). Female and non-br. male are a drab mottled brown and buff with dark stripes on the head, but male in this plumage still shows a red bill. In this obscure

Southern Tchagra E

Larger than similar Brown-crowned Tchagra with a much stronger and more robust bill. Also has a darker crown edge and has darker and greyer underparts. Confusion should not arise with Brown-crowned Tchagra because it is very unlikely they would ever occur together. Forages on the ground, scraping leaf litter with its bill and feet to expose prey items. **Habitat**: Coastal scrub, forest edges and thickets. **Status**: Common. **Voice**: Song, given in aerial display, is 'wee-chee-chee-cheee', descending in pitch. (Grysborsttjagra)

17–21 cm | Br: Mar, Aug–Nov J F M A M J J A S O N D

Grey-headed Bush-Shrike

A much larger version of the Orange-breasted Bush-Shrike with a more massive, hooked bill, a pale, not dark eye and lacking yellow forehead and eye-stripe. Shows a white area at base of bill towards eye. Juv. has variable amounts of orange on breast, from just a slight wash to deep orange. **Habitat**: Thickets in acacia savanna and broad-leaved woodland. **Status**: Common. **Voice**: Drawn-out 'ooooooop' (hence colloquial name 'Ghostbird'); 'tic-tic-ooooop'. (Spookvoël)

24–26 cm | Br: Apr, Jul–Feb J F M A M J J A S O N D

Bokmakierie E

This robust shrike is a familiar bird in many areas and its call is commonly heard. The ad. is easily recognised by its grey head, green back and bright yellow underparts with a black gorget. Imm. lacks the black gorget, but the undertail, like that of the ad., has conspicuous yellow tips that are obvious in flight. Display consists of head bowing and tail raising by both ads as they face each other. **Habitat**: Shrublands, Karoo scrub, grassland with scattered bushes and suburban gardens. **Status**: Common. **Voice**: Very varied whistles, but usually duetted 'bok-bok-kik'. (Bokmakierie)

22–23 cm | Br: Jan–Dec J F M A M J J A S O N D

Orange-breasted Bush-Shrike

Most similar to Grey-headed Bush-shrike but very much smaller and with a less robust bill. It further differs by having an orangey-yellow, not grey-and-white forehead and eyebrow stripe and a dark, not yellow eye. Juv. is duller than ad. and lacks the yellow on the head. **Habitat**: Acacia savanna and riverine forests. **Status**: Common. **Voice**: Song is frequently repeated 'poo-poo-poo-pooooo', fading towards end; deeper 'pu pu pu pu'; harsher 'titit-eeezz'. (Oranjeborsboslaksman)

16–18 cm | Br: Aug–Mar J F M A M J J A S O N D

GLOSSARY

Breeding endemic A species that breeds in a particular region but migrates during the non-breeding season.

Call Short notes given by males and females for alarm and contact purposes (*see also* Song).

Cap Area encompassing the forehead and crown.

Casque A helmet or helmet-like structure on the bill.

Cere Coloured, bare skin at the base of the upper mandible (in raptors).

Colonial Associating in close proximity, while roosting, feeding or nesting.

Crest Elongated feathers on the forehead, crown or nape.

Cryptic Pertaining to camouflage coloration.

Decurved Curving downwards.

Display A pattern of behaviour in which the bird attracts attention while it is defending territory or courting a female, for example.

Endemic Restricted to a certain region.

Eye-ring Circle of coloured feathers immediately behind the eye.

Feral Species that have escaped from captivity and now live in the wild.

Flush To rouse and put to flight.

Immature A bird that has moulted its juvenile plumage but has not yet attained full adult plumage.

Juvenile The first full-feathered plumage of a young bird.

Migrant A species that undertakes long-distance flights between its wintering and breeding areas.

Malar stripes Lines running from the base of the bill to the sides of the throat (see illustration).

Moustachial stripes Lines running from the base of the bill to the sides of the head (see illustration).

Parasitise To lay eggs in the nest of another species for the purposes of incubation.

Pelagic Living in open oceans or seas.

Plumage Feathers of a kind.

Primaries The outermost major flight feathers of the wing.

Resident A bird that occurs throughout the year in a region and is not known to undertake migration.

Roost To sleep or rest, either in flocks or singly.

Secondaries Flight feathers of the wing, adjoining the primary feathers.

Shield Bare patch of skin at the base of the bill and on the forehead. Often brightly coloured.

Song A series of notes given by the male to proclaim his territory (*see also* Call).

Summer visitor A bird that is absent from the region during winter.

Territory An area that a bird establishes and defends from others.

Vent Area from the belly to the undertail coverts.

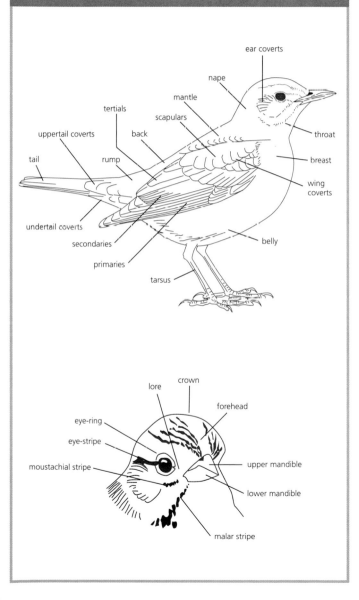

PARTS OF A BIRD

Black-browed Albatross

Ad. resembles a large Kelp Gull with much longer, straighter wings. Ad. has white underwing with very broad black borders and this, combined with a yellowish, orange-tipped bill, is diagnostic. Imm. has predominantly dark underwing with a grey, black-tipped bill, smoky smudges on head and an incomplete greyish collar. **Habitat**: Open ocean, breeding at subantarctic islands; scavenges at trawlers. **Status**: Common year round, but ad. mostly May–Oct. Sometimes ventures close inshore along the S and W Cape coasts. **Voice**: Grunts and squawks. (Swartrugalbatros)

81–95 cm | Br: n/a | J F M A M J J A S O N D

Atlantic Yellow-nosed Albatross

Smaller and more slender than Black-browed Albatross and has white underwing narrowly bordered with black. The bill appears totally black but at close range a yellow stripe is evident on the upper ridge. Differs from Indian Yellow-nosed Albatross by having grey, not grey-cheeked white head. Imm. lacks yellow on bill. **Habitat**: Open ocean, breeding at Tristan da Cunha and Gough islands. **Status**: Fairly common year round in small numbers. **Voice**: Generally silent at sea. (Atlantiese geelneusalbatros)

72–80 cm | Br: n/a | J F M A M J J A S O N D

Southern Giant Petrel

Large, albatross-like seabird with thickset body, hunched back and large, thick, hooked bill. White-chinned Petrel is very much smaller and blacker overall, with much thinner wings. Colour is variable, from deep chocolate-brown to greyish with paler head to a white version dotted with black spots. **Habitat**: Open ocean; breeds at subantarctic islands. Scavenges at trawlers and around seal colonies. **Status**: VULNERABLE. Fairly common in coastal waters, but decreasing in numbers. **Voice**: Harsh grunts and wheezes when squabbling over food. (Reusenellie)

86–99 cm | Br: n/a | J F M A M J J A S O N D

White-chinned Petrel

Considerably larger than Sooty Shearwater, is much darker brown, appearing almost black, and lacks silvery underwing. Diagnostic pale bill and white chin can be seen at close range. Wings long and narrow; has a towering, careening flight action high above waves. **Habitat**: Open ocean; breeds at subantarctic islands. Most abundant in shelf waters, where it scavenges at trawlers. **Status**: VULNERABLE. Common year round, but probably decreasing due to longline fishing. **Voice**: High-pitched 'titititititi' when squabbling over food. (Bassiaan)

51–58 cm | Br: n/a | J F M A M J J A S O N D

Subantarctic Skua

Large brown seabird that resembles an imm. Cape Gull but lacks the white rump and shows conspicuous white patches at the base of the primaries. This bird, the largest member of the skua family, has a heavy body, broad-based wings and mottled brown plumage. Some birds show a tawny head and throat. Flight is normally slow and ponderous but when chasing another seabird to pirate its prey, it thrusts forward on powerful wings. **Habitat**: Open ocean; regularly scavenges at trawlers. **Status**: Common migrant in S. **Voice**: Generally silent. (Bruinroofmeeu)

60–66 cm | **Br: n/a** | J F M A M J J A S O N D

Sooty Shearwater

Smaller and paler than White-chinned Petrel and has diagnostic silvery underwing. Flight is swift and direct with rapid wing beats interspersed with glides when bird banks over waves and flashes its silvery underwings. On migration, very large concentrations of these birds come close inshore along the W Cape coast. They feed in mixed flocks with Cape Gannets and Cape Cormorants. **Habitat**: Open ocean, especially in coastal waters; breeds on subantarctic islands. **Status**: Common to abundant. **Voice**: Silent at sea. (Malbaartjie)

40–46 cm | **Br: n/a** | J F M A M J J A S O N D

Great Shearwater

A much more patterned seabird similar to Cory's Shearwater. Chief difference between the two is this species' obvious black cap and white collar, dusky belly patch and dark lines on underwing and an all-dark not dark-tipped yellow bill. The upperparts are not uniform and show a patterned, scaly effect with dark feathers edged greyish. **Habitat**: Open ocean; breeds at Tristan da Cunha and Gough islands. **Status**: Fairly common Oct–Mar, scarce Jun–Jul. **Voice**: Silent at sea. (Grootpylstormvoël)

46–53 cm | **Br: n/a** | J F M A M J J A S O N D

Cory's Shearwater

Most likely to be confused with similar-sized Great Shearwater but is more uniform brown on upperparts and lacks a white collar and black cap. Also much whiter on the underparts and lacks dusky underwing markings and dusky belly patch. Bill is yellowish with dark tip. **Habitat**: Open ocean; breeds at islands in N Atlantic and Mediterranean. Often forages in association with dolphins and tuna. **Status**: Common Palaearctic migrant, mostly Oct–Apr. **Voice**: Silent at sea. (Geelbekpylstormvoël)

45–53 cm | **Br: n/a** | J F M A M J J A S O N D

Antarctic Prion

Prions are notoriously difficult to identify in the field but this is the prion most commonly encountered around the coast. Features common to all prions are the blue-grey upperparts with an open 'W' across the back and wings, a dark-tipped tail and white underparts. **Habitat**: Open ocean; breeds at subantarctic islands and Antarctica. **Status**: Common visitor, mostly late May–Aug, occurring in large flocks. Subject to 'wrecks' when large numbers of dead and dying birds come ashore. **Voice**: Silent at sea. (Antarktiese walvisvoël)

25–28 cm | **Br:** n/a   J F M A M **J J A** S O N D

Wilson's Storm-Petrel

During winter, the most common storm-petrel in the area. In summer could be confused with European Storm-Petrel but is larger with more rounded wings and has dark, not white on the underwing. Its feet project beyond the tail in flight. Its long legs and toes dangle and patter the water's surface when feeding. **Habitat**: Open ocean, breeding at subantarctic islands and Antarctica; may occur at high densities, but seldom flocks; often follows ships. **Status**: Common year round in S; more abundant May–Sep; uncommon elsewhere. **Voice**: Silent at sea. (Gewone stormswael)

15–19 cm | **Br:** n/a   J F M A **M J J A S** O N D

European Storm-Petrel

Smaller than Wilson's Storm-Petrel and differs chiefly by showing a white stripe on the underwing and not having its feet project beyond the tail's end in flight. Its flight is much more rapid than Wilson's Storm-Petrel, with bat-like movements and often quick dashes to and fro. Storm-petrels seen in large flocks during summer are usually of this species. Often seen in groups resting on the ocean. **Habitat**: Open ocean. **Status**: Common summer visitor. Attends trawlers. **Voice**: Silent at sea. (Europese stormswael)

14–17 cm | **Br:** n/a   J F M A M J J A **S O N D**

Pintado Petrel

An easily identifiable, conspicuous seabird. The chequered black-and-white upperparts are diagnostic; the underparts are predominantly white with a dark throat. Flight very floppy for a seabird but, in stronger winds, it glides and turns, twisting from side to side. **Habitat**: Open ocean; breeds on subantarctic and Antarctic islands. Habitually follows trawlers. Does not venture close to shore except during storms. **Status**: Common visitor to coastal waters, mostly Apr–Oct. **Voice**: High-pitched 'cheecheecheechee' when feeding. (Seeduifstormvoël)

38–40 cm | **Br:** n/a   J F M **A M** J J **A S O** N D

White-breasted Cormorant

By far the largest of the cormorants. Has a clear white breast and throat and, in the breeding season, white thigh patches. Imm. has variable amount of white on breast and belly and is best distinguished from Reed Cormorant by its much larger size. Differs from similarly sized African Darter by having a much thicker neck, broader head and shorter tail. Coastal birds avoid feeding over the open ocean, preferring sheltered bays and estuaries. **Habitat**: Coastal and fresh waters. **Status**: Locally common. **Voice**: Grunts and squeals at colonies; otherwise silent. (Witborsduiker)

80–100 cm | **Br: Jan–Dec** J F M A M J J A S O N D

Bank Cormorant   E

Might be confused with Cape Cormorant but is larger and has duller, less shiny plumage, thicker, woolly-necked appearance and lacks any naked yellow skin at base of bill. It also has a slight rounded crest and when breeding shows various amounts of white on head and rump. **Habitat**: Rocky shores, islands and stacks; seldom moves more than 10 km from breeding islands. **Status**: VULNERABLE. Locally common, but decreasing in numbers. **Voice**: Wheezy 'wheeee' at nest; otherwise silent. (Bankduiker)

76 cm | **Br: Jan–Dec** J F M A M J J A S O N D

Cape Cormorant   BrE

Most abundant marine cormorant of the region. Sometimes vast numbers can be seen from the shore as they fly in straight lines or skeins to and from their feeding areas. Ad. is a glossy, bluish-black with a conspicuous orange throat patch. Imm. is a dowdy brownish colour and lacks the white underparts of the larger White-breasted Cormorant. **Habitat**: Coastal waters, estuaries and lagoons. Often feeds and roosts in huge flocks. **Status**: Abundant, but numbers decreasing. **Voice**: 'Gaaaa' and 'geeee' noises at nest; otherwise silent. (Trekduiker)

61–65 cm | **Br: Jan–Dec** J F M A M J J A S O N D

Crowned Cormorant   E

The marine equivalent of the Reed Cormorant, from which it differs by having a longer tuft of feathers on the forehead, a shorter tail and a brighter orange-red face. Juv. differs from Reed Cormorant by having a dark, not pale breast and belly. Usually found in small groups or singly away from br. colonies. Spends long periods out of water with wings outstretched. **Habitat**: Offshore islands, coast, estuaries and lagoons. **Status**: Locally common. **Voice**: Cackles and hisses at colonies; otherwise silent. (Kuifkopduiker)

50–55 cm | **Br: Jan–Dec** J F M A M J J A S O N D

Reed Cormorant

Most often seen with White-breasted Cormorant and African Darter, from which it is distinguished by being much smaller. Ad. in br. plumage has a barred back, orange face and throat, and a small erectile crest. Tail is proportionately longer and more graduated than that of White-breasted Cormorant. Imm. is brownish-grey with white underparts. Often seen perched with wings outstretched on a prominent post over water. **Habitat:** Lakes, dams and rivers; also sheltered coastal waters outside S Africa. **Status:** Common. **Voice:** Cackles and hisses at colonies; otherwise silent. (Rietduiker)

50–55 cm | Br: Jan–Dec   J F M A M J J A S O N D

African Darter

Resembles a cormorant but has a thin, almost snake-like head and neck, and a long, stiletto-shaped bill. Sides of head and neck are rufous and mantle and wing coverts are streaked with buff. When swimming, the body is held submerged with only the neck and head showing; neck is held curved and moves backwards and forwards as the bird swims. Imm. has a white head that darkens with age. **Habitat:** Lakes, dams and slow-moving rivers; rarely coastal lagoons and estuaries. **Status:** Common. **Voice:** Croaks when breeding; otherwise silent. (Slanghalsvoël)

80 cm | Br: Jan–Dec   J F M A M J J A S O N D

Great White Pelican

This large bird can be confused only with the smaller Pink-backed Pelican but the ad. is much whiter and has contrasting black flight feathers and a brighter yellow pouch. Imm. is much larger and a darker brown than imm. Pink-backed Pelican. Frequently flies in 'V' formation. **Habitat:** Groups feed by herding shoals of fish and then scooping them up in their large bills. Nests colonially on ground. **Status:** Locally common. The only pelican in the Cape coastal area. **Voice:** Usually silent; deep 'mooo' given at breeding colonies. (Witpelikaan)

140–178 cm | Br: Jan–Dec   J F M A M J J A S O N D

Pink-backed Pelican

Noticeably smaller than Great White Pelican and much drabber grey; never as crisply white. Flight feathers do not contrast strongly with greyish wings and body and, in flight, underwings appear uniform in colour. Bill pouch is grey or pink, not yellow as in Great White Pelican. Imm. darker than ad. but never as dark brown as imm. Great White Pelican. **Habitat:** Lakes and estuaries; typically fishes alone; nests colonially in trees. **Status:** Locally common. Occurrence virtually restricted to KwaZulu-Natal coastal estuaries and freshwater lakes. **Voice:** Usually silent. (Kleinpelikaan)

135–152 cm | Br: Jun–Sep, Dec–Jan   J F M A M J J A S O N D

Kelp Gull E

The largest gull in the region. The ad. is easily identified by its white body, jet black back and upperwings and bright yellow bill with an orange spot at the tip. Imm. plumage is very variable but in the first year the bird is very dark brown with a pale rump; it becomes paler with age. **Habitat**: Coast and adjacent wetlands; follows trawlers up to 100 km from shore. Increasingly found on fields up to 50 km inland. **Status**: Common. **Voice**: Loud 'ki-ok'; short, repeated alarm call, 'kwok'. (Swartrugmeeu)

juv.

55–65 cm | Br: Sep–Feb   J F M A M J J A S O N D

Sabine's Gull

A small marine gull with a buoyant, almost tern like flight. The strikingly tricoloured wing pattern and shallowly forked white tail are diagnostic. At close range the non-br. ad. shows a black bill with a yellow tip. In imm. the bill is all black. **Habitat**: Pelagic but closer to shore in storms and large sheltered bays. **Status**: Common summer visitor, often in flocks. **Voice**: Silent in the region. (Mikstertmeeu)

non-br.

27–32 cm | Br: n/a   J F M A M J J A S O N D

Grey-headed Gull

Differs from Hartlaub's Gull by having a dove-grey head, pale eye and bright red bill, legs and feet. It is also slightly larger bodied and has a longer, heavier bill than Hartlaub's. Imm. Grey-headed Gull has more extensive dark markings on the head, paler legs, a pink bill with a dark tip and a more extensive black tip to the tail than imm. Hartlaub's. **Habitat**: Open coast, and coastal and freshwater wetlands. Breeds inland, away from the sea. **Status**: Locally common. **Voice**: Typical 'karrh' and 'pok-pok'. (Gryskopmeeu)

imm.

40–42 cm | Br: Feb–Nov   J F M A M J J A S O N D

Hartlaub's Gull E

Slightly smaller than Grey-headed Gull with a darker red bill and legs, and dark eyes. In br. plumage shows a faint grey hood, but in non-br. plumage has a completely white head. Imm. has faint brownish markings on the head, the black tip to the tail is either reduced or absent, and it has a brown, not two-tone bill as in imm. Grey-headed Gull. **Habitat**: Inshore waters, coastline, estuaries, urban areas and flooded fields. **Status**: Common. This is the small gull common along the S Cape coast. **Voice**: Drawn-out, rattling 'kaaarrh' and 'pok-pok'. (Hartlaubmeeu)

36–38 cm | Br: Apr–Sep   J F M A M J J A S O N D

African Penguin   E

The black-and-white face pattern is diagnostic. General upright stance and black-and-white plumage render it unmistakable when seen ashore. At sea it swims low in the water with only the neck and head breaking the surface. Imm. is dark greyish-blue and lacks head pattern of ad. When moving fast through water, it 'porpoises' regularly. **Habitat**: Coastal; rare beyond 50 km from shore. **Status**: VULNERABLE. Most common on S and W coasts where it breeds on offshore islands, but numbers decreasing. **Voice**: Loud, donkey-like braying, especially at night. (Brilpikkewyn)

60–70 cm | **Br:** Jan–Dec   J F M A M J J A S O N D

Cape Gannet   BrE

Differs from the large albatrosses by being whiter, having a long, dagger-shaped bill and a long, pointed tail. Imm. is dark brown version of ad. and differs from White-chinned Petrel by fine speckling on back, its pale belly and much larger size. When feeding, plunges into sea from considerable height with partly folded wings. Seen regularly from shore in all weathers, sometimes as it gathers in large feeding flocks. **Habitat**: Coastal waters; often feeds at trawlers. **Status**: VULNERABLE. **Voice**: Noisy 'warrra-warrra-warrra' at colonies and when feeding at sea. (Witmalgas)

87–100 cm | **Br:** Jul–Jan   J F M A M J J A S O N D

Caspian Tern

The largest tern in the world, it is instantly recognisable by its conspicuous coral-red bill. In br. plumage has totally black cap but non-br. and imm. plumage has the cap streaked black and white. Imm. has an orange bill and dark-edged back feathers. In flight the shallowly forked tail and the black tips to the underside of the primaries can be seen. **Habitat**: Virtually any large wetland and sheltered coastal waters. **Status**: Locally common breeding resident. **Voice**: Deep, harsh 'kraaak'; imm. gives a weak, nasal whistle. (Reusesterretjie)

47–54 cm | **Br:** Jul–Aug, Dec–Jan   J F M A M J J A S O N D

Lesser Crested Tern

Confusable with Swift Tern but is noticeably smaller and is paler grey above; also has a shorter, more slender bill which is orange, not yellowish-green. Juv. is similar to juv. Swift Tern but is smaller and has an orange bill. Usually found in mixed tern roosts on beaches, but forages offshore, sometimes at great distance. **Habitat**: Inshore waters, bays and estuaries. **Status**: Common summer migrant along E coast. **Voice**: Hoarse 'kreck'. (Kuifkopsterretjie)

35–37 cm | **Br:** n/a   J F M A M J J A S O N D

Common Tern
During summer, the most abundant small tern on the southern African coast. Has many features in common with most small, non-br. terns (grey upperparts, white underparts, and a partially developed black cap). Subtle aids to identification are the long, slightly decurved bill and uniform grey rump. **Habitat**: Coastal waters and adjacent wetlands. **Status**: Abundant Palaearctic migrant, mostly Oct–Apr, but some imm. year round. Often forms vast roosting flocks on beaches and at river mouths. **Voice**: 'Kik-kik' and 'kee-arh'. (Gewone sterretjie)

31–35 cm | **Br: n/a** | J F M A M J J A S O N D

non-br.

Arctic Tern
Very difficult to tell apart from Common Tern but differs by having a shorter, spiky bill and much shorter legs. In flight is daintier than Common Tern and has a white, not grey rump and has paler, almost translucent wing tips. Differs from Antarctic Tern by having black, not deep red bill. **Habitat**: Pelagic; sometimes roosts ashore, usually with Common Tern. **Status**: Fairly common passage migrant along W coast, rare on E coast and vagrant inland. **Voice**: Short 'kik-kik' in flight. (Arktiese sterretjie)

33–35 cm | **Br: n/a** | J F M A M J J A S O N D

non-br.

Antarctic Tern
A dumpier, more thickset tern than both Arctic and Common terns and has a bill of varying shades of red, not black. The bill is also thicker and more robust. Shows varying amount of grey on the underparts and has an obvious white cheek stripe in br. plumage. **Habitat**: Coastal waters to shelf-break; often roosts ashore. **Status**: Fairly common migrant from Antarctica and subantarctic, mostly May–Sep. **Voice**: Sharp, high-pitched 'kik-kik'. (Grysborssterretjie)

34–36 cm | **Br: n/a** | J F M A M J J A S O N D

non-br.

Swift Tern
Smaller than the Caspian Tern, this species has a yellow, not red bill. At long range it shows a plain white underwing. In br. plumage has black cap ending just before the bill, imparting a white forehead; when not breeding has variable amount of black on forehead but appears mostly white or grizzled. Imm. has mottled upperparts and extensive black on head but still shows yellow bill. **Habitat**: Coastal waters, estuaries and coastal wetlands. **Status**: Common resident and local migrant. **Voice**: Ad.'s call is harsh 'kree-eck'; juv. gives thin, vibrating whistle. (Geelbeksterretjie)

46–49 cm | **Br: Feb–Oct** | J F M A M J J A S O N D

Damara Tern   BrE

Confusable with Little Tern but in br. plumage has a black, not white forehead. In non-br. and imm. plumage when it has a white forehead it is best told apart from Little Tern by its uniform grey upperparts, lacking the white tail and rump. The bill is slightly longer and slightly decurved. **Habitat**: Sheltered coastlines, bays and lagoons; breeds South Africa (scarce) to Namibia. **Status**: Locally common intra-African migrant. **Voice**: Far-carrying, rapid 'chit-ick', higher pitched than Little Tern's. (Damarasterretjie)

23 cm | Br: Sep–Apr   J F M A M J J A S O N D

White-winged Tern

Most abundant small freshwater tern in our area. Non-br. plumage is pale grey and white with small amounts of black on the head and underwing. In br. plumage (seldom seen in the region) the bird is a striking contrast of black, grey and white, with the silvery forewings being most noticeable. Flight can be almost butterfly-like and is very buoyant as the bird dips over water to pick up food. **Habitat**: Lakes, estuaries and marshes; occasionally forages in sheltered bays on coast and over open country. **Status**: Common Palaearctic migrant. **Voice**: Short 'kek-kek'. (Witvlerksterretjie)

non-br.

20–23 cm | Br: n/a   J F M A M J J A S O N D

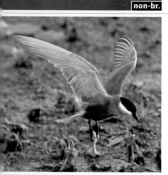

Whiskered Tern

Unmistakable in br. plumage with dark grey body, and black cap contrasting with very obvious white whiskers. In non-br. plumage it is easily confused with White-winged Tern but is larger, more heavily built and has a more robust, thicker bill. It also has a grey, not white rump and a more grizzled head pattern. **Habitat**: Most wetlands and marshes, but requires floating vegetation to breed. **Status**: Fairly common resident and Palaearctic migrant. **Voice**: Repeated, hard 'zizz'. (Witbaardsterretjie)

25–26 cm | Br: Oct–Apr   J F M A M J J A S O N D

Little Tern

This tiny tern is unmistakable in br. plumage when it shows a diagnostic white forehead and a yellow bill with black tip. In non-br. plumage it differs from similar non-br. Damara Tern by invariably showing yellow legs and feet and has a white, not grey rump and tail. **Habitat**: Shallow coastal waters and estuaries. **Status**: Fairly common summer migrant. **Voice**: Slightly rasping 'ket-ket'. (Kleinsterretjie)

non-br.

22–24 cm | Br: n/a   J F M A M J J A S O N D

Little Grebe

One of the smallest aquatic birds in the region. Sides of head are chestnut during br. season (diagnostic). Non-br. birds are drab greyish-brown; in all plumages a pale spot at base of bill is diagnostic. In flight the Little Grebe has very rapid wing beats and shows a white wing stripe and a bright white belly. Frequently dives; often will emerge with just the head showing to watch intruder. **Habitat**: Lakes, dams and other freshwater bodies; rarely in estuaries and sheltered bays. **Status**: Common resident. **Voice**: Noisy; distinctive whinnying trill. (Kleindobbertjie)

23–29 cm | Br: Jan–Dec JFMAMJJASOND

imm.

Great Crested Grebe

A large grebe with gleaming white breast and foreneck with diagnostic double crest and a face edged with a rufous ruff. Non-br. birds have much reduced rufous ruff and a whiter face. Juv. has a striped head pattern. Rarely seen in flight but does show obvious white forewings and white trailing edge to the secondaries. **Habitat**: Large lakes and pans; rarely in estuaries and sheltered bays. **Status**: Locally common. **Voice**: Barking 'rah-rah-rah'; various growls and snarls. (Kuifkopdobbertjie)

45–56 cm | Br: Jan–Dec JFMAMJJASOND

Black-necked Grebe

Differs from the smaller Little Grebe in non-br. plumage by having white, not dark cheeks, throat and foreneck. Br. plumage has the head and neck sooty black with conspicuous orange ear patches. At close range, a bright, button-like, cherry-red eye is obvious. When not breeding, sometimes gathers in large flocks at coastal lagoons and salt works; often at sea in sheltered bays. **Habitat**: Lakes, pans and occasionally sheltered bays. **Status**: Fairly common, but localised resident and nomad. **Voice**: Mellow trill during display. (Swartnekdobbertjie)

28–33 cm | Br: Oct–Apr JFMAMJJASOND

Spur-winged Goose

Readily distinguished by its large size, black-and-white pied plumage, and pinkish legs and bill. Male has a fleshy pink knob on the forehead. Female and imm. are dull brown and have less white in the plumage. Out of the br. season the birds gather in large flocks on open stretches of water and moult their flight feathers, which renders them flightless for several weeks. **Habitat**: Wetlands and adjacent grassland and fields. **Status**: Common. **Voice**: Feeble, wheezy whistle in flight. (Wildemakou)

75–100 cm | Br: Jan–Dec JFMAMJJASOND

Egyptian Goose

The chestnut eye patch, white forewings and dark patch on the breast are diagnostic. When not breeding, occurs in fairly large flocks in open fields, on dams, or on sand bars in rivers. In flocks they tend to be noisy and aggressive, attacking each other and giving loud honking and hissing noises. **Habitat**: Wetlands and adjacent grassland and fields; also suburban areas and sheltered bays on coast. **Status**: Very common. **Voice**: Male hisses; female utters grunting honk; both honk repeatedly when alarmed or taking flight. (Kolgans)

63–73 cm | **Br**: Jan–Dec   J F M A M J J A S O N D

South African Shelduck   E

Male has a grey head and neck while female shows a white face and black neck. In flight both show large conspicuous white forewings similar to Egyptian Goose but differ by having rufous-coloured body. **Habitat**: Freshwater lakes and dams in drier areas; nests in hole in ground. **Status**: Common, gathering in large flocks to moult after breeding. **Voice**: Various honks and hisses. (Kopereend)

64 cm | **Br**: May–Sep   J F M A M J J A S O N D

Knob-billed Duck

A large black-and-white duck in which the male has a large black knob on its bill that increases in size when breeding. The head is white speckled with black. In flight the wings are totally black and contrast with a pale grey rump. **Habitat**: Pans and lakes in woodland and along larger rivers; nests in tree holes. **Status**: Locally common nomad and intra-African migrant. **Voice**: Whistles, but usually silent. (Knobbeleend)

56–76 cm | **Br**: Sep–Apr   J F M A M J J A S O N D

White-faced Whistling Duck

The white face (sometimes stained), chestnut breast and barred flanks help identify this duck. The stance is also characteristic: the body is held very upright and the neck is stretched to its full length. **Habitat**: Freshwater lakes and lagoons, and adjacent grassland. **Status**: Common, often in large flocks. **Voice**: The call is a three-part whistle 'wee-wee-weeoo' and is often heard at night when flocks move from one feeding ground to another. (Nonnetjie-eend)

43–48 cm | **Br**: Aug–May   J F M A M J J A S O N D

Fulvous Whistling Duck

Similar in shape to White-faced Duck but has a rich golden head and body with bright white flank stripes. In flight shows a white rump that contrasts strongly with dark tail and back. Sometimes occurs in large flocks, often in company with White-faced Duck. Often dives when foraging. **Habitat**: Freshwater lakes and dams. **Status**: Locally common, but generally less abundant than White-faced Duck. **Voice**: Soft, disyllabic whistle. (Fluiteend)

43–53 cm | **Br**: Jan–Dec | J F M A M J J A S O N D

African Pygmy Goose

A tiny duck with orange breast and flanks, a bright yellow bill, white face and dark green back. Male has green face and neck patches bordered with black. In flight shows conspicuous white wing patches. **Habitat**: Freshwater lakes with floating vegetation, especially Nymphaea lilies; nests in hole in tree. **Status**: Locally common. **Voice**: Soft, repeated 'tsui-tsui'. (Dwerggans)

30–33 cm | **Br**: Sep–May | J F M A M J J A S O N D

Southern Pochard

Sits low in the water and, on take-off, runs across the water before gaining flight. Habitually dives. Male is distinguished by its dark plumage, blue bill and bright red eye. Female is brown with a pale patch at the base of the bill and a pale crescentic mark on the sides of the face. In flight both sexes show a pale belly and have a broad white strip running down the centre of the wing. **Habitat**: Lakes and dams, including alkaline lakes. **Status**: Common. **Voice**: Male makes whining sound; female quacks. (Bruineend)

48–51 cm | **Br**: Jan–Dec | J F M A M J J A S O N D ♀

Yellow-billed Duck

The rich, almost chrome-yellow bill, which has a black, wedge-shaped patch on top, is diagnostic of this mottled brown duck. When the wings are unfolded in flight they show at the base a brilliant blue and green patch (the speculum) that is bordered with black and white. **Habitat**: Freshwater lakes, ponds and flooded fields; also lagoons and estuaries. **Status**: Common; often occurs in flocks. **Voice**: Male gives rasping hiss; female quacks. (Geelbekeend)

51–58 cm | **Br**: Jan–Dec | J F M A M J J A S O N D

African Black Duck

A dark, sooty-black duck with white speckles on the back, dark bill and orange legs and feet. Wing pattern similar to Yellow-billed Duck but bluer and has white, not grey wing linings. Sits very low in the water and appears very long bodied. **Habitat**: Streams and rivers; less frequent on ponds and dams. Pairs defend territories along rivers, so seldom occurs in flocks. **Status**: Fairly common. **Voice**: Female gives a sharp 'quack', especially in flight; male gives weak, high-pitched whistle. (Swarteend)

48–57 cm | Br: Jan–Dec | J F M A M J J A S O N D

Cape Shoveler   E

Distinguished from Yellow-billed Duck by its black bill, which is spatulate and appears longer than the head. Other identifying features are the bright orange legs and the powder-blue forewings, which are very conspicuous in flight. Female is duller than male, has a darker head and a smaller patch of blue on the forewings. **Habitat**: Freshwater lakes and ponds. **Status**: Common. Occurs in small groups on fresh water, often in company with Yellow-billed Ducks. **Voice**: Female call is a 'quack'; male call is continuous rasping. (Kaapse slopeend)

53 cm | Br: Jan–Dec | J F M A M J J A S O N D

Cape Teal

Smaller than Yellow-billed Duck and easily identified by its mottled greyish plumage and slightly upturned pink bill. In flight the wing pattern shows two broad white stripes bordering a small green speculum. Differs from Red-billed Teal by lacking the dark cap of that species. **Habitat**: Fresh or saline wetlands, especially alkaline lakes, saltpans, lagoons and sewage works. **Status**: More common in the drier areas of the region, particularly on saline lagoons and lakes. **Voice**: The call is a high-pitched nasal whistle, which is mostly given in flight. (Teeleend)

44–48 cm | Br: Jan–Dec | J F M A M J J A S O N D

Red-billed Teal

This medium-sized brown and buff mottled duck is easily recognised by its creamy cheeks, which contrast with a dark cap and reddish bill. In flight it shows a buff speculum. **Habitat**: Freshwater wetlands. **Status**: Common. Out of the br. season, this duck gathers in substantial flocks, sometimes with other species. **Voice**: Male gives soft, nasal whistle; female quacks. (Rooibekeend)

43–48 cm | Br: Jan–Dec | J F M A M J J A S O N D

Hottentot Teal

A small duck that vaguely resembles the Red-billed Teal but differs by having a blue, not red bill and dark ear patches on its buffy face. In flight shows broad white trailing edge to secondaries and extensive white on the underwings. **Habitat**: Freshwater wetlands, favouring areas with emergent or floating vegetation. **Status**: Locally common; typically in pairs or small flocks. **Voice**: Generally silent; utters high-pitched quacks when taking flight. (Gevlekte eend)

30–35 cm | **Br:** Jan–Dec J F M A M J J A S O N D

White-backed Duck

A small, rather grebe-like duck with a pale spot at base of bill, characteristic humped back and large head. Body is barred rufous and dark brown; white back is visible only in flight. An excellent diver, is seldom seen in flight, and spends much of day roosting with head tucked into scapulars. **Habitat**: Fresh water, typically among floating vegetation. **Status**: Locally common. **Voice**: Low-pitched whistle, rising on second syllable. (Witrugeend)

38–40 cm | **Br:** Jan–Dec J F M A M J J A S O N D

Maccoa Duck

The only stiff-tailed duck in the region. Br. male has chestnut body, black head and heavy blue bill. Female and eclipse male are dark brown, with pale stripe under eye and paler throat, giving head striped appearance (unlike female Southern Pochard, which has a pale crescent behind the eye). Sits very low in water, with stiff tail often cocked at 45° angle. In flight, upperwing is uniform dark brown. **Habitat**: Freshwater lakes, dams and lagoons. **Status**: Locally common, but sparsely distributed. **Voice**: Peculiar, nasal trill. (Bloubekeend)

48–51 cm | **Br:** Jan–Dec J F M A M J J A S O N D

Red-knobbed Coot

A medium-sized, matt black, duck-like bird with an ivory-white bill and unfeathered forehead. The two red knobs situated on the top of the white shield are more conspicuous during the br. season but are only noticeable at close range. Imm. is similar to imm. Common Moorhen but is larger and greyer in appearance, and lacks the white undertail coverts. Sometimes found in large flocks; dives regularly to feed. **Habitat**: Dams, lakes and virtually any wetland except fast-flowing rivers. **Status**: Common to abundant. **Voice**: Harsh, metallic 'claak'. (Bleshoender)

41–46 cm | **Br:** Jan–Dec J F M A M J J A S O N D

Black Crake
A small, furtive bird with matt black coloration, a yellow bill and red eyes and legs. Imm. is a greyish-brown version of ad. and has a dark bill and dull red legs. A noisy bird, more often heard than seen. More inclined to venture from cover into the open at dawn and dusk, when it may be seen darting over floating vegetation. **Habitat:** Marshes with dense reed beds; sometimes at small ponds. **Status:** Common. Often bold, foraging out in open. **Voice:** Throaty 'chrrooo'; hysterical, bubbling, wheezy duet. (Swartriethaan)

18–20 cm | Br: Jan–Dec | J F M A M J J A S O N D

African Jacana
A rufous bird with a dark belly, white throat and breast and yellow foreneck. The black-and-white head pattern, which offsets a blue frontal shield and bill, is diagnostic. The toes and toenails, which are exceptionally elongated to allow walking on floating vegetation, are conspicuous. Imm. is duller, with a paler head and underparts. On landing, this species often holds its wings open over its back. **Habitat:** Wetlands with floating vegetation, especially water lilies. **Status:** Common. **Voice:** Noisy; sharp, ringing 'krrrek'. (Grootlangtoon)

28–31 cm | Br: Jan–Dec | J F M A M J J A S O N D

Common Moorhen
Smaller than African Purple Swamphen, which it resembles in that it has a red frontal shield, but this species has a yellow tip to the bill and has green, not red legs and toes. Plumage is sooty-black but there is a diagnostic white stripe on flanks, and outer undertail coverts are white. Swims with jerky movements and constant flicking of tail on open water. Imm. is greyish-brown version of ad. **Habitat:** Wetlands with fringing vegetation; bolder than other gallinules, often swimming in open water. **Status:** Common to abundant. **Voice:** Sharp 'krrik'. (Grootwaterhoender)

30–36 cm | Br: Jan–Dec | J F M A M J J A S O N D

African Swamphen
This large, reed-dwelling bird has a bright purplish-blue head and underparts, and a green back offset by bright white undertail coverts. Large bill and frontal shield are bright red, as are legs and long toes. When creeping about in reed beds it flicks its tail up and down, revealing the white undertail coverts. In flight the legs and toes project well beyond the tail, giving a heron-like outline. **Habitat:** Reed beds, marshes and flooded grassland. **Status:** Common. **Voice:** Variety of harsh shrieks, wails and booming notes. (Grootkoningriethaan)

33–46 cm | Br: Jan–Dec | J F M A M J J A S O N D

Yellow-billed Egret

Smaller than Great White Egret with a shorter and thicker neck that is never held in such a pronounced 'S' shape. When breeding the bill becomes more orange, not black as in Great White Egret and the tops of the legs turn a lurid yellowish-green. Told apart from much smaller Little Egret by having black, not yellow toes. **Habitat**: Marshes and flooded grassland; rarely at estuaries. **Status**: Common resident and nomad. **Voice**: Typical heron-like 'waaaark'. (Geelbekwitreier)

61–69 cm | **Br**: Jan–Dec   J F M A M J J A S O N D

Great Egret

Much larger than similar Yellow-billed Egret and has a much longer and thinner neck which is usually held in a kinked 'S' shape. Differs further when breeding by having a black, not orangey bill and lacks the greenish-yellow tops of the legs. When breeding, develops long, elaborate plumes on head and lower back. **Habitat**: Lakes, dams, estuaries and lagoons. **Status**: Common. **Voice**: Low, heron-like 'waaaark'. (Grootwitreier)

85–92 cm | **Br**: Jan–Dec   J F M A M J J A S O N D

non-br.

Little Egret

A small white 'heron' with a black bill and diagnostic yellow toes. Habitually frequents shallows in freshwater and estuary areas where it feeds by dashing to and fro, repeatedly stabbing at its prey. During this frenzied feeding activity the yellow toes can often be seen. In br. plumage shows wispy white head plumes and lace-like aigrettes on the lower back. **Habitat**: Wetlands, coastal pools, mangroves and estuaries. **Status**: Common. **Voice**: Harsh 'waaark'. (Kleinwitreier)

56–65 cm | **Br**: Jan–Dec   J F M A M J J A S O N D

Western Cattle Egret

The white 'heron' seen following cattle or game. The br. bird has a buffy crown, breast and back, and reddish legs; the non-br. and imm. birds are white with brownish or greenish legs. Smaller than other white 'herons', and the most gregarious away from breeding colonies, often forming flocks that follow cattle. They fly to their roosts in tight 'V' formations. **Habitat**: Mostly in grassland, often in association with cattle or game; roosts in large trees or reed beds. **Status**: Common; highly gregarious. **Voice**: Heron-like 'aaaark' or 'pok-pok'. (Veereier/Bosluisvoël)

50–56 cm | **Br**: Aug–Apr   J F M A M J J A S O N D

Goliath Heron

Its large size is diagnostic and it is the largest heron in the world. In colour it most closely resembles the Purple Heron, which is very much smaller and has stripes on the head and has yellow, not dark legs. The flight is very slow and ponderous and shows deep chestnut wing linings. **Habitat**: Lakes, dams, large rivers and estuaries, usually where there are extensive reeds or papyrus. **Status**: Locally common. **Voice**: Loud, low-pitched 'kwaaark'. (Reusereier)

120–152 cm | **Br**: Jan–Dec   J F M A M J J A S O N D

Purple Heron

Superficially resembles Goliath Heron but is very much smaller and the rufous head and neck are boldly striped black. Juv. and imm. lack the grey nape and mantle of ad. and are less streaked on the neck with less extensive black on the crown. In flight the long neck is held tucked into the body; appears overall very dark in colour. **Habitat**: Wetlands, typically among sedges and reeds; seldom forages in the open. **Status**: Common. **Voice**: Hoarse 'kraaark'. (Rooireier)

79–84 cm | **Br**: Jan–Dec   J F M A M J J A S O N D

Grey Heron

A large, long-legged grey bird, often seen standing motionless in water while fishing. Closer inspection reveals a yellow, dagger-shaped bill and a white head with black eye-stripe that ends in a wispy crest. Imm. lacks black eye-stripe and crest, and is duller in colour. In flight can be distinguished from Black-headed Heron by having a uniform grey underwing. It flies with the head and neck tucked tightly into the shoulders. **Habitat**: Pans, dams, slow-flowing rivers, lagoons and estuaries. **Status**: Common. **Voice**: Harsh 'kraaunk' in flight. (Bloureier)

90–100 cm | **Br**: Jan–Dec   J F M A M J J A S O N D

Black-headed Heron

The black top of the head and hind neck contrast with the white throat and render this heron unmistakable. Imm. has the black on the head and neck replaced with grey and could be confused with imm. Grey Heron but, like the ad., it has contrasting black-and-white underwings. **Habitat**: Grassland, fields and scrubland; also marsh fringes, but seldom forages in water. **Status**: Common. **Voice**: Loud 'aaaaark'; various hoarse cackles and bill clapping at nest. (Swartkopreier)

84–92 cm | **Br**: Jan–Dec   J F M A M J J A S O N D

Squacco Heron

Variable plumage from all streaked to plain buff. Streaked plumage is very bittern-like but has all-white wings. In flight the buff or streaked body plumage contrasts strongly with the all-white wings. When breeding the nape feathers are elongated plumes. **Habitat**: Vegetated margins of lakes, pans and slow-moving rivers; skulks in long grass, sitting motionless for long periods. **Status**: Common. **Voice**: Low-pitched 'kruuk'; rattling 'kek-kek-kek'. (Ralreier)

48–46 cm | Br: Jan–Dec | J F M A M J J A S O N D

Black Heron

When feeding, its habit of forming an 'umbrella' by raising its wings over its head and stretching forward is diagnostic. The legs are black with bright yellow toes, similar to Little Egrets. Juv. is slightly paler than ad.'s sooty-black plumage. Encountered sometimes in large foraging groups, which work together herding fish. **Habitat**: Lakes and marshes; occasionally estuaries. **Status**: Locally common resident and nomad. **Voice**: Seldom calls; deep 'kraak'. (Swartreier)

48–50 cm | Br: Aug–Apr | J F M A M J J A S O N D

Black-crowned Night Heron

A squat, small, grey-and-white heron with a black back, cap and hind neck. Very often seen hunched and hiding deep within tangles of trees during the day. Juv. is very bittern like, being heavily streaked and spotted and is greyish-brown, not tawny in colour. In flight the ad.'s black back contrasts with grey wings. **Habitat**: Lakes, rivers and rocky shores. **Status**: Common resident. **Voice**: Harsh 'kwok' in flight. (Gewone nagreier)

56–61 cm | Br: Aug–Apr | J F M A M J J A S O N D

imm.

Green-backed Heron

This small, dark grey heron is unmistakable with its black crown, pale blue-grey underparts, grey mantle and scalloped, patterned wing coverts. The legs are a bright orangey-yellow. Juv. is streaked brown and buff and at rest might be confused with juv. Squacco Heron but lacks white wings. **Habitat**: Sluggish rivers overhung with trees, lake shores (often in rocky areas), mangroves and coral reefs at low tide. **Status**: Fairly common. **Voice**: Sharp 'baaek' when flushed. (Groenrugreier)

40 cm | Br: Jan–Dec | J F M A M J J A S O N D

Abdim's Stork

A black-and-white stork, considerably smaller than the White Stork with which it often associates. Distinguished from all other similar storks by its diagnostic white lower back. At close range, the blue face and greyish legs with red joints are noticeable. Often occurs in very large flocks in agricultural lands. **Habitat**: Grassland and fields, often in company with White Storks. **Status**: Common intra-African migrant; more abundant in some years than in others. **Voice**: Usually silent; weak, two-note whistle at nests and roosts. (Kleinswartooievaar)

76–81 cm | **Br: n/a**   J F M A M J J A S O N D

White Stork

A large, white, heron-like bird with contrasting black flight feathers and bright red bill. Legs are also bright red but become covered in excrement and appear greyish-white. Imm. similar to ad. except its bill and legs are duller red and white plumage is dusted with brown. **Habitat**: Grassland and fields; occasionally at shallow wetlands. **Status**: Common Palaearctic migrant, mostly Oct–Apr. A few pairs breed in W Cape, S Africa. **Voice**: Silent except on nest, when loud whining and bill clapping are given. (Witooievaar)

102–120 cm | **Br: Sep–Nov**   J F M A M J J A S O N D

Yellow-billed Stork

The combination of red face and very long, slightly decurved yellow bill is diagnostic. When breeding the face becomes a deep red and the wings are tinged with pink. Can be confused with White Stork in flight but has a yellow, not red bill and a black, not white tail. Juv. is heavily mottled grey and brown with a dull greenish-grey bill. **Habitat**: Lakes, rivers and estuaries. **Status**: Common resident and partial intra-African migrant. **Voice**: Normally silent except during br. season, when it gives loud squeaks and hisses. (Nimmersat)

91–105 cm | **Br: Mar Jun–Oct**   J F M A M J J A S O N D

Marabou Stork

This huge bird is virtually confined to game reserves, where it is seen soaring over the bush or scavenging at a kill with vultures. The enormous bill, unfeathered head and neck, and naked, pink fleshy pouch render this bird unmistakable. Its wingspan approaches that of the Wandering Albatross, the world's longest at almost 2 m. **Habitat**: Savanna, grassland and wetlands; often around towns; also at refuse dumps and abattoirs. Breeds colonially in trees. **Status**: Fairly common resident or local migrant. **Voice**: Low, hoarse croak when alarmed; claps bill when displaying. (Maraboe)

150–155 cm | **Br: May–Oct Dec**   J F M A M J J A S O N D

Saddle-billed Stork

This huge black-and-white stork is unmistakable. The long, thick red-and-black banded bill with a yellow saddle at the base is diagnostic. Male has brown eye, female yellow. Juv. is a duller version of ad. and lack bill's saddle. Ponderous and slow flight shows a bold black-and-white pattern on both surfaces of the wings. **Habitat**: Freshwater dams, lakes and rivers. **Status**: Uncommon; usually solitary or in pairs. Undertakes seasonal movements in some areas. **Voice**: Normally silent except for bill clapping during display. (Saalbekooievaar)

145 cm | Br: Jan–Aug   J F M A M J J A S O N D

African Openbill

Large black stork with diagnostic wide nutcracker-like gap between the mandibles. The bill is dark over its length, paling to grey at the base. Mantel and breast feathers are elongate and when wet appear curly. Juv. is a duller version of ad. and the bill's nutcracker-like gap develops with age. **Habitat**: Freshwater lakes and dams, where it feeds mostly on snails and mussels. **Status**: Locally common intra-African migrant; breeds mostly S of equator. **Voice**: Seldom heard; croaking 'honk'. (Oopbekooievaar)

81–94 cm | Br: Aug–May   J F M A M J J A S O N D

Woolly-necked Stork

Only at close range can the fuzzy-shaped 'woolly' white feathers be seen on the neck. Face has a black patch around eyes and the bill has a reddish tip. Combination of glossy black plumage contrasting with white belly and undertail and rump all help in identification. Juv. is very much duller and the white neck less woolly and the head has a dark cap. **Habitat**: Wetlands, often along rivers and streams; also mangroves, coastal mudflats and reefs. **Status**: Uncommon; resident and intra-African migrant. **Voice**: Seldom heard; harsh croak. (Wolnekooievaar)

85 cm | Br: Aug–Dec   J F M A M J J A S O N D

African Spoonbill

From a distance, it looks like a white, egret-type bird but when seen at close range, the long, flattened, spoon-shaped grey-and-red bill is diagnostic. The legs, feet and face are bright red. Unlike egrets and herons, it flies with neck outstretched, and the silhouette of the spoon-shaped bill can be seen. Imm. is duller and has dark-tipped flight feathers. When feeding, scythes its spatulate bill from side to side through water. **Habitat**: Lakes, flood plains and estuaries. **Status**: Common resident and local migrant. **Voice**: Low 'kaark' at breeding colonies. (Lepelaar)

90 cm | Br: Jan–Dec   J F M A M J J A S O N D

Hadeda Ibis

A dull, greyish-brown bird with long legs and a long, decurved bill. At close range an iridescent bronze patch is conspicuous on the shoulder and the faint dark and pale lines that run under the eye can be seen. Bill is dark brown but has an almost translucent red ridge. In flight it gives its distinctive 'ha-ha, ha-ha, de-da' call from which it derives its name. **Habitat**: Forest clearings, woodland, savanna, grassland, farmland and lawns. Usually in small parties; roosts in trees. **Status**: Common. **Voice**: Noisy on flights to and from roosts: loud 'ha-de-da'. (Hadeda)

76–89 cm | **Br: Jun–Mar**   J F M A M J J A S O N D

Southern Bald Ibis   E

Not likely to be confused with smaller Bald Ibis in that its head is featherless and shows a bald red-and-white pattern and a long, red, not dark decurved bill. Juv. is a much duller version of ad. and lacks the bold head pattern. In flight the wings appear long and narrower than other dark ibises. **Habitat**: Short grassland, often in burned areas; breeds colonially on cliffs. **Status**: VULNERABLE. Locally common resident. Occurs in flocks. **Voice**: High-pitched, wheezing call. (Kalkoenibis)

78 cm | **Br: Jul–Nov**   J F M A M J J A S O N D

Glossy Ibis

A small, very slender ibis, appearing almost black when seen at long range. Ad. when seen close up shows deep chestnut wings and body with the back glossy deep green with purple highlights. Juv. shows some glossy regions of plumage but is overall much duller. In flight the neck appears longer and thinner than other dark-coloured ibises. **Habitat**: Lakes, dams, pans, estuaries and flooded grassland. **Status**: Locally common. **Voice**: Normally silent; low, guttural 'kok-kok-kok' when breeding. (Glansibis)

55–65 cm | **Br: Jul–Apr**   J F M A M J J A S O N D

African Sacred Ibis

A predominantly white bird with a black head and neck that at close range can be seen to be unfeathered. In flight a narrow black border to the trailing edge of the wings is visible. During the br. season shows a stripe of bare scarlet skin on leading edge of underwing. Imm. resembles ad. but head and neck feathered white. **Habitat**: Open habitats, from offshore islands, wetlands and fields to grassland. **Status**: Common. **Voice**: Loud croaking at breeding colonies. (Skoorsteenveër)

64–82 cm | **Br: Jan–Dec**   J F M A M J J A S O N D

Greater Flamingo

Larger and paler than the Lesser Flamingo: when seen feeding together, this species almost dwarfs the Lesser Flamingo. As a general rule, the Greater is much whiter, having the pink confined to the wings. The pink bill with a black tip is diagnostic. Imm. differs from imm. Lesser Flamingo by being much larger and having a more massive bill. **Habitat**: Shallow lakes, saltpans, lagoons and sandy beaches; feeds on large prey filtered from bottom sediments. **Status**: Common resident, intra-African migrant and nomad. **Voice**: Noisy, goose-like honking. (Grootflamink)

127–140 cm | Br: Jan–Dec   J F M A M J J A S O N D

Lesser Flamingo

Much smaller than Greater Flamingo and almost always much redder than that species. Imm. and some pale ads have pale plumage but their smaller size and the diagnostic deep red bill, which at a distance looks black, should rule out confusion. The Lesser and Greater flamingos feed in the same manner: with the head submerged upside down as they filter food through the trough-like bill. **Habitat**: Lakes, saltpans and estuaries. **Status**: Common resident, intra-African migrant and nomad. **Voice**: More muted honking than Greater Flamingo's. (Kleinflamink)

81–90 cm | Br: Jan–Dec   J F M A M J J A S O N D

Black-winged Stilt

This wader is distinguished by the combination of its exceptionally long pink legs and its black-and-white plumage. The bill is long, black, very thin and pointed. Female and imm. have the black on the back and wings tinged with brown; imm. has extensive brown markings on its hindneck and head. Br. male shows a black nape and crown. **Habitat**: Most wetlands, both fresh- and saltwater. **Status**: Common nomadic resident. **Voice**: Harsh, short 'kik-kik', especially when alarmed; very vocal in defence of nest and young. (Rooipootelsie)

38 cm | Br: Jan–Dec   J F M A M J J A S O N D

Pied Avocet

An unmistakable, large black-and-white wader with a long, very thin, upturned bill. The legs are long and blue and the feet are partly webbed. In flight the three black patches in each wing make a very striking pattern. Frequents lakes and vleis where the birds regularly swim, dipping their heads and bills under water. **Habitat**: Most wetlands and occasionally along coast. **Status**: Common nomadic resident and Palaearctic migrant in N; usually in small flocks. **Voice**: Clear 'kooit'; 'kik-kik' alarm call. (Bontelsie)

43 cm | Br: Jan–Dec   J F M A M J J A S O N D

African (Black) Oystercatcher

E

A medium-sized black wader with an obvious orange-red bill, dull pink legs and a bright orange ring around the eye. Imm. is dowdier and has a less vividly coloured bill. When in flight the bird appears all black and has no wing markings, although a few individuals may show some white on the underparts. **Habitat**: Coastline, estuaries and lagoons. **Status**: Common from C Namibia to E Cape; locally common in S Angola; vagrant to S Mozambique. **Voice**: 'Klee-kleeep'; fast 'peeka-peeka-peeka' alarm call. (Swarttobie)

44 cm | Br: Sep–Apr | J F M A M J J A S O N D

Ruddy Turnstone

Can be seen running over pebbly beaches or poking about in strands of rotting seaweed. Bill is short, slightly flattened and upturned. Upperparts are dark and pale underparts show irregular dark markings on the front and sides of the breast. Legs are relatively short and are bright orange with darker joints. In flight it shows heavily patterned wings and tail. **Habitat**: Rocky shores and estuaries, occasionally on sandy shores and coastal lagoons; rare inland. **Status**: Common Palaearctic migrant, mostly Oct–Apr. **Voice**: Hard 'kttuck', especially in flight. (Steenloper)

non-br.

21–24 cm | Br: n/a | J F M A M J J A S O N D

Ruff

Rich buff edging to mantle feathers imparts a scaly pattern and a variable amount of buff on underparts help identify this shore bird. Leg colour is variable but usually greenish; can range from bright yellow to orange. Some males in non-br. plumage show a white head and neck. The full br. plumage is never seen in Africa. **Habitat**: Most wetlands; also forages in dry fields. Often swims in deep water. **Status**: Common Palaearctic migrant, mostly Sep–Apr. **Voice**: Generally silent; occasional 'tooi' flight note. (Kemphaan)

♀

♂ 30 cm
♀ 24 cm | Br: n/a | J F M A M J J A S O N D

Red Knot

A fairly nondescript grey shore bird with short legs and dumpy shape. Longer billed and smaller than Grey Plover and has a uniform, not patterned back. Differs from smaller Curlew Sandpiper by its shorter bill and in flight has grey, not white rump. In br. plumage underparts are a deep chestnut red. **Habitat**: Estuaries and coastal lagoons; occasionally inland. **Status**: Locally common Palaearctic migrant to W and S coast, mostly Sep–Apr; vagrant elsewhere. **Voice**: Soft 'knut'. (Knoet)

non-br.

23–25 cm | Br: n/a | J F M A M J J A S O N D

Common Ringed Plover

A small, short-legged, dark shore bird with bright orange legs, white collar and a dark brown or black breast band which is often incomplete in non-br. plumage. Bill is short and blunt and often shows an orange base. Forages singly with slow, deliberate movements, dashing forward suddenly to peck at prey. **Habitat**: Coastal and inland wetlands, preferring patches of soft, fine mud. **Status**: Common Palaearctic migrant, mostly Sep–Apr. **Voice**: Fluty, rising 'too-li'. (Ringnekstrandkiewiet)

non-br.

18–20 cm | Br: n/a | J F M A M J J A S O N D

Three-banded Plover

This small plover has an overall elongated appearance and frequently bobs its head and tail. The double black breast band is diagnostic; this species also shows a grey face and throat, red eye-ring and red base to the bill. Although it occurs singly or in pairs on smaller stretches of water, at certain times of the year large numbers may gather at favoured freshwater dams. **Habitat**: Wetland fringes, preferring fresh water **Status**: Common. **Voice**: Penetrating, high-pitched 'weee-weet' whistle. (Driebandstrandkiewiet)

18 cm | Br: Jan–Dec | J F M A M J J A S O N D

Kittlitz's Plover

This small plover is distinguished by its cinnamon-coloured underparts and by the black line on the forehead that extends behind the eye onto the nape. Imm. lacks the black head markings of ad. but is darker than similar White-fronted Plover and has a dark shoulder mark. **Habitat**: Fields, short grassland and fringes of wetlands. **Status**: Common resident and local nomad. Not often seen on open beaches; it occurs in small flocks sometimes far from water. **Voice**: Short, clipped trill, 'kittip'. (Geelborsstrandkiewiet)

14–15 cm | Br: Jan–Dec | J F M A M J J A S O N D

Chestnut-banded Plover

A very small, very pale grey shore bird. Male shows a distinct narrow chestnut breast band and a variable amount of chestnut on the head. Female has a duller, less defined chestnut breast band. Juv. very similar to ad. but has a faint grey breast band. **Habitat**: Saltpans and soda lakes, estuaries and coastal wetlands. **Status**: Fairly common resident and local nomad. **Voice**: Single 'prrp' or 'tooit'. (Rooibandstrandkiewiet)

15 cm | Br: Jan–Dec | J F M A M J J A S O N D

White-fronted Plover

A small, pale plover likely to be confused with imm. Kittlitz's Plover but this species generally has a paler breast, a much paler, sandier coloured back and a black marking on the forehead. Imm. lacks dark marking on head and is paler than ad., with buff edging to feathers of the back and mantle. **Habitat**: Coastline, estuaries and larger inland rivers and pans. **Status**: Common. **Voice**: Clear 'wiiit'; 'tukut' alarm call. (Vaalstrandkiewiet)

16 cm | Br: Jan–Dec   J F M A M J J A S O N D

Sanderling

A small, very pale grey shore bird with a dark patch on the folded forewing. In flight shows a broad white wing bar and a dark centre to the tail. When feeding on beaches, it typically chases after receding waves and is the only shore bird to do this. Br. plumage shows back a richly spangled white, reddish and black with reddish throat and breast. **Habitat**: Mainly sandy beaches; also rocky shores and coastal wetlands; rare inland. **Status**: Common Palaearctic migrant, mostly Sep–Apr. **Voice**: Single, decisive 'wick'. (Drietoonstrandloper)

non-br.   38–45 cm | Br: n/a   J F M A M J J A S O N D

Little Stint

A tiny shore bird and easily identified on size alone. Typically feeds in flocks and has a rapid feeding action, almost sewing machine-like as it stabs at food on the muddy surface. Br. plumage has the face, throat and breast turn a deep chestnut. Flocks in flight display amazing turn and twist manoeuvres with a follow-my-leader action. **Habitat**: Estuaries, lagoons and freshwater wetlands. **Status**: Common Palaearctic migrant, mostly Oct–Apr. **Voice**: Short, sharp 'schit'. (Kleinstrandloper)

non-br.   13–15 cm | Br: n/a   J F M A M J J A S O N D

Greater Sand-plover

Larger than vaguely similar White-fronted Plover, with a bigger body, longer legs and a longer, more robust bill. In br. plumage has a rufous breast band. Leg colour is variable but usually grey-green (very rarely black). Imm. Kittlitz's Plover is overall more buffy and is smaller. Juv. has buff-fringed upperparts. **Habitat**: Chiefly coastal wetlands. **Status**: Locally common Palearctic migrant to E coast; rarer in W. **Voice**: Soft trilled 'tirrrri'. (Grootstrandkiewiet)

non-br.   **br.**   22–25 cm | Br: n/a   J F M A M J J A S O N D

Curlew Sandpiper
A small wading bird with longish legs and a long, decurved bill. Appears very grey in the field; in flight shows a broad white rump and a noticeable wing bar. Br. plumage is totally different: rufous underparts and brightly patterned upperparts, but the whitish rump is still evident. Feeds by walking belly-deep in water and probing its bill into mud. **Habitat**: Found in a wide variety of wetland habitats, but is most common in coastal estuaries. **Status**: Common summer visitor. **Voice**: A short trill, 'chirrup'. (Krombekstrandloper)

18–23 cm | Br: n/a | J F M A M J J A S O N D

non-br.

Common Sandpiper
This small, usually solitary wader has a peculiar habit of bobbing backward and forward between short bursts of running. It is uniformly drab brown above and white below, with the white on the breast curving up and over the shoulder. In flight the wings are held slightly bowed downwards and are flicked rapidly between short glides. **Habitat**: Wetlands and along coast. **Status**: Common Palaearctic migrant, mostly Sep–Apr. **Voice**: Flight call is a shrill 'ti-ti-ti', higher pitched and thinner than Wood Sandpiper's. (Gewone ruiter)

19–21 cm | Br: n/a | J F M A M J J A S O N D

Wood Sandpiper
Has a bobbing action similar to that of Common Sandpiper but not as exaggerated. Identification points are the brownish back, well spotted with buff or white, the white rump and barred tail (best seen in flight), a pale grey underwing, and long greenish-yellow legs which project well beyond the tail in flight. **Habitat**: Freshwater wetlands. **Status**: Common Palaearctic migrant, mostly Sep–Apr. **Voice**: Highly vocal; high-pitched, slightly descending 'chiff-iff-iff'. (Bosruiter)

19–21 cm | Br: n/a | J F M A M J J A S O N D

Terek Sandpiper
A small, short-legged, dumpy wader with a long, upturned bill. Teeters much like Common Sandpiper but when feeding, frantically dashes and zigzags when chasing crab prey. In flight shows white trailing edge to wings and the bright orangey-yellow legs are conspicuous. **Habitat**: Muddy estuaries and lagoons, especially mangroves and areas with eel-grass (Zostera). **Status**: Common Palaearctic migrant, mostly Oct–Apr. **Voice**: Series of fluty, uniformly-pitched 'weet-weet-weet' notes. (Terekruiter)

22–25 cm | Br: n/a | J F M A M J J A S O N D

 ### Marsh Sandpiper

Confusable with Common Greenshank but is smaller, overall paler with proportionally longer, thinner legs and a much thinner, straight black bill. In br. plumage the back has more mottling and the neck is more streaked. Feeds solitarily in shallow water, but will swim in deeper areas when it might be confused with a phalarope. **Habitat**: Wetlands. **Status**: Common Palaearctic migrant, mostly Oct–Mar. **Voice**: High-pitched 'yeup', often repeated; higher pitched and less strident than Common Greenshank's. (Moerasruiter)

| non-br. |

22–25 cm | Br: n/a | J F M A M J J A S O N D

 ### Grey Plover

Medium-sized wading bird that is drab grey, lightly speckled with white above, and off-white to white below. Head is relatively large and bill is short and black. Only in flight are the diagnostic black armpits clearly visible. In br. plumage (rarely seen in the region) the underparts are jet black and the upperparts are spangled with silver. When feeding, these birds remain motionless and then dart forward to pick up their prey. **Habitat**: Coast and adjacent wetlands. **Status**: Common Palaearctic migrant, mostly Aug–Apr, but many year round. **Voice**: Clear 'tluuii'. (Grysstrandkiewiet)

| non-br. |

28–31 cm | Br: n/a | J F M A M J J A S O N D

 ### Common Greenshank

A medium-sized, very grey wader with a slightly upturned, dark-tipped grey bill and long, greyish-olive legs. In flight it shows a conspicuous white rump that extends up the back in a white wedge. It is often seen running around in the shallows chasing small fish. **Habitat**: Coastal and freshwater wetlands. **Status**: Common Palaearctic migrant, mostly Oct–Apr, but many year round. **Voice**: Loud, slightly rasping 'chew-chew-chew'. (Groenpootruiter)

30–35 cm | Br: n/a | J F M A M J J A S O N D

 ### Bar-tailed Godwit

This large wader is easily recognised by its very long, upturned bill, the basal half of which is pink. The non-br. bird is mottled grey and brown above and white below, but in br. plumage the underparts assume a rich orange-brown colour. In flight it shows a white rump and finely barred tail, and dark upperwings. **Habitat**: Estuaries and coastal lagoons; rare inland. **Status**: Fairly common Palaearctic migrant, especially along the W coast, mostly Oct–Apr. Sometimes gathers in large groups to roost. **Voice**: 'Wik-wik' or 'kirrik' call, often given in flight. (Bandstertgriet)

| non-br. |

38 cm | Br: n/a | J F M A M J J A S O N D

Common Whimbrel

From a distance it might be confused with Bar-tailed Godwit but this bird has a long, decurved bill. At closer range the diagnostic black stripes on the head, bisected by a pale stripe down the centre of the crown, and the pale eye-stripe can be seen. In flight it shows a conspicuous white rump that extends onto the lower back. **Habitat**: Coastal wetlands and, to a lesser extent, open shores; scarce inland. **Status**: Common Palaearctic migrant, mostly Oct–Apr, but many year round. **Voice**: Bubbling, whistled 'whiri-iri-iri-iri-iri'; highly vocal in non-br. season. (Kleinwulp)

40 43 cm | Br: n/a | J F M A M J J A S O N D

Eurasian Curlew

Could be confused with the smaller Common Whimbrel but lacks the head stripes of that species and has a proportionately much longer, decurved bill. Female is larger than male and has a longer bill. Juv. has a shorter bill but is paler than Common Whimbrel and lacks the head stripes. **Habitat**: Large estuaries and lagoons; scarce inland. **Status**: Fairly common Palaearctic migrant, mostly Oct–Apr. **Voice**: Loud 'cur-lew'. (Grootwulp)

53–59 cm | Br: n/a | J F M A M J J A S O N D

Spotted Thick-knee

Cryptically-coloured wading bird with a large head and big yellow eyes. Bill is short and yellow at its base and the legs are greenish-yellow. Plumage is mottled brown, buff and black and in flight shows two small white patches in the upperwing. When defending its territory, the wings are held fully spread and slightly forward to display the white wing patches. **Habitat**: Virtually any open country, including fields and parks. **Status**: Common resident; often in pairs. **Voice**: Rising then falling 'whi-whi-whi-WHI-WHI-WHI-whi-whi', usually at night. (Dikkop)

43 cm | Br: Aug–Apr | J F M A M J J A S O N D

Water Thick-knee

Slightly smaller than Spotted Thick-knee and easily told apart by showing an obvious pale grey wing panel and a streaked, not spotted breast. As its name suggests, is more often associated with wetlands than Spotted Thick-knee. Chiefly nocturnal but more often seen active in daytime than Spotted Thick-knee. **Habitat**: River and lake shores with suitable cover. **Status**: Common resident; usually in pairs. **Voice**: Rather mournful 'ti-ti-ti-tee-teee-tooo', slowing and dropping in pitch at end, usually at night. (Waterdikkop)

38–41 cm | Br: Jul–Jan | J F M A M J J A S O N D

African Snipe

A very long-billed, heavily patterned shore bird. The plumage is highly cryptic with rich dark brown and buff barring, streaking and blotching making it extremely well camouflaged. Has a jerky zigzag flight when flushed. **Habitat**: Marshes and flooded grassland, usually in muddy areas with short vegetation. **Status**: Common resident and local nomad. **Voice**: Sucking 'scaap' when flushed; males produce whirring, drumming sound with their stiffened outer-tail feathers during aerial display flights. (Afrikaanse snip)

30–32 cm | Br: Mar–Oct | J F M A M J J A S O N D

Hamerkop

The hammer-shaped profile of the head and bill render it unmistakable. Tail is finely barred. In flight it might be mistaken for a bird of prey were it not for its long bill and the legs projecting beyond the tail. Normally associated with water where it wades in the shallows, searching for frogs. **Habitat**: Lakes, dams and rivers. Nest is huge, domed structure of sticks, with small side entrance, usually in sturdy tree or on cliff ledge. **Status**: Common. **Voice**: Sharp 'kiep' in flight; jumbled mixture of querulous squawks and frog-like croaks during courtship. (Hamerkop)

48–56 cm | Br: Jan–Dec | J F M A M J J A S O N D

Crowned Lapwing

A very familiar wader not associated with water but commonly encountered in towns and villages where it frequents grassy road verges and open sports fields. Readily identified by its brownish plumage with a white belly and the diagnostic black cap surrounded by a white 'halo'. The bird's legs are bright vermilion, as is the bill base. **Habitat**: Open country; not associated with water. Favours short grassland, fields and fallow land. **Status**: Common; regularly found with Black-winged Lapwing. **Voice**: Noisy; loud, grating 'kreep', day and night. (Kroonkiewiet)

30–31 cm | Br: Jan–Dec | J F M A M J J A S O N D

Black-winged Lapwing

Similar to Senegal Lapwing but is larger and more heavily built, shows more white on the forehead which extends almost to the eyes, and has a broader black border separating the breast from the belly, especially in the male. In flight shows black, not white triangular patches on secondaries and has a white bar running across the wing coverts. **Habitat**: Highland and lowland grassland. **Status**: Fairly common resident and local migrant. **Voice**: Shrill, piping 'ti-reee', higher pitched than Senegal Lapwing. (Grootswartvlerkkiewiet)

26–27 cm | Br: Jul–Oct | J F M A M J J A S O N D

Senegal Lapwing

Most likely to be confused with Black-winged Lapwing but is slightly smaller and less stocky, has a narrower black border to the lower breast, much reduced white on the forehead and slight greenish tinge to the mantle. In flight the upper- and underwings show a white triangular patch on the secondaries. **Habitat**: Open, short grassy savanna, often in recently burned areas. **Status**: Uncommon resident and local migrant. **Voice**: Clear double-note 'tee-oo'. (Kleinswartvlerkkiewiet)

22–26 cm | **Br**: Aug–Nov   J F M A M J J A S O N D

White-crowned Lapwing

A large lapwing with distinctive pendulous, yellow wattles and yellow legs. May be mistaken for the African Wattled Lapwing because of its white (not brown) breast. White-crowned Lapwing is also identified by a white stripe running from the forehead to the nape. In flight the wings are predominantly white with only the outer primaries and inner coverts being black. **Habitat**: Wetland margins and adjacent grassland. **Status**: Fairly common. **Voice**: High pitched, ringing 'keep-keep'; regularly calls at night. (Witkopklewiet)

30 cm | **Br**: Mar, Jul–Nov   J F M A M J J A S O N D

African Wattled Lapwing

The largest lapwing of the region. It has smaller yellow wattles than the White-crowned Lapwing, and a dark, not white breast that is bordered by a black band and a streaked, not plain grey neck. In flight lacks the startling white wings of White-crowned Lapwing but does show a white wing bar. **Habitat**: Wetland margins and adjacent grassland. **Status**: Fairly common. **Voice**: High-pitched, ringing 'keep-keep'; regularly calls at night. (Lelkiewiet)

35 cm | **Br**: Jul–Jan   J F M A M J J A S O N D

Blacksmith Lapwing

This large black, white and grey bird is the easiest lapwing (plover) to identify and the bold wing pattern makes it readily distinguishable in flight. Imm. is a duller version of ad. with brown feathering replacing the black. When alarmed and put to flight the bird gives a rapid, metallic 'tink tink' call. **Habitat**: Wetland margins and adjoining grassland and fields. **Status**: Common; often in flocks when not breeding. **Voice**: Very vocal; loud, ringing 'tink, tink, tink' alarm call. (Bontkiewiet)

31 cm | **Br**: Jan–Dec   J F M A M J J A S O N D

Temminck's Courser

Smaller than similar Burchell's Courser and differs chiefly in lacking a greyish-blue patch on the nape and has a broad, not narrow black patch on the belly. In flight lacks white trailing edge to secondaries and white tips to outer tail. Usually in pairs or family groups, but sometimes in flocks on recently burned areas. **Habitat**: Dry, sparsely grassed and recently burned areas. **Status**: Locally common nomad and intra-African migrant. **Voice**: Grating 'keerkeer'. (Trekdrawwertjie)

19–21 cm | **Br:** May–Jan   J F M A M J J A S O N D

Burchell's Courser   E

Most likely confused with smaller Temminck's Courser but has a greyish-blue nape patch and a narrow, not broad black bar on the belly. In flight shows a narrow white, not black trailing edge to the secondaries and a white tip to the outer tail. Difficult to detect in some habitats due to its excellent camouflage. Usually in pairs or family groups; rarely in flocks. **Habitat**: Dry, sparsely grassed plains, arid regions and open fields. **Status**: Uncommon nomad and intra-African migrant. **Voice**: Harsh, repeated 'wark'. (Bloukopdrawwertjie)

23 cm | **Br:** Jul–Apr   J F M A M J J A S O N D

Double-banded Courser

The two narrow black bands running across the upper breast are diagnostic. Head pattern has a dark cap contrasting with buffy eyebrow stripe. The back pattern is heavily scalloped with greyish feathers broadly edged with pale creamy buff. White rump is conspicuous in flight, as are the chestnut panels on the secondaries and part primaries. **Habitat**: Semi-arid and desert plains, usually in stony areas. **Status**: Common resident. **Voice**: Thin, falling and rising 'teeu-wee' whistle; repeated 'kee-kee', mostly at night. (Dubbelbanddrawwertjie)

20–24 cm | **Br:** Jan–Dec   J F M A M J J A S O N D

Bronze-winged Courser

A large, rather robust courser with distinctive head and breast markings. Violet-tipped primaries are not a field character. In flight, white uppertail coverts and wing bars contrast with dark upperparts. Juv. has rufous-tipped feathers on upperparts. **Habitat**: Woodland and savanna. Largely nocturnal; roosts under bushes during the day. **Status**: Fairly common resident and intra-African migrant. **Voice**: Ringing 'ki-kooi' at night. (Bronsvlerkdrawwertjie)

26–28 cm | **Br:** Jul–Dec   J F M A M J J A S O N D

Red-billed Spurfowl NE

A medium-sized spurfowl, overall greyish and finely barred on the underparts. Combination of reddish bill and legs with dull yellow bare skin around the eyes is diagnostic. **Habitat**: Arid savanna and open, broad-leaved woodland, often in thickets along watercourses. **Status**: Locally common; easily observed; less skulking than other spurfowl. **Voice**: Loud, harsh 'chaa-chaa-chek-chek' at dawn and dusk. (Rooibekfisant)

35–38 cm | Br: Jan–Dec | J F M A M J J A S O N D

Swainson's Spurfowl NE

This large brown spurfowl is easily distinguished by having bare red skin around the eyes and on the throat and this, combined with its dark brown legs, is diagnostic. Sexes are similar and imm. is a dowdier version of the ad. **Habitat**: Dry savanna and fields. **Status**: Common; usually in groups of 3–6 birds. **Voice**: Raucous 'krraae-krraae-krraae' by males at dawn and dusk. (Bosveldfisant)

38 cm | Br: Nov–May | J F M A M J J A S O N D

Red-necked Spurfowl

Might be confused with Swainson's Spurfowl but has red, not dark brown legs and has much more boldly patterned underparts. Very variable throughout its range with varying amounts of black-and-white patterning on underparts. **Habitat**: Forest edges, thickets, riparian scrub and adjoining grassland. **Status**: Common. **Voice**: Loud 'kwoor-kwoor-kwoor-kwaaa' at dusk and dawn. (Rooinekfisant)

36 cm | Br: Nov–Jul | J F M A M J J A S O N D

Cape Spurfowl E

This large game bird is the spurfowl most frequently seen in fynbos in the S Cape. At a distance it appears a uniform greyish-brown with a dark cap but at close range the plumage is finely vermiculated with grey and buff. Sexes are similar and imm. is browner than ad. Occurs in pairs or small groups and is reluctant to take flight, preferring to run off and hide in undergrowth. **Habitat**: Lowland fynbos, pastures, fields, large gardens and riparian thickets in Karoo. **Status**: Common; often confiding. **Voice**: Loud, ringing 'cackalac-cackalac-cackalac'. (Kaapse fisant)

42 cm | Br: Aug–Mar | J F M A M J J A S O N D

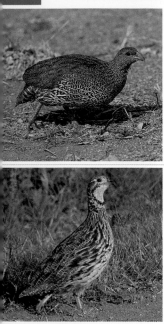

Natal Spurfowl   NE

A drab and fairly uniform spurfowl with scaly-patterned underparts and orangey bill and dull reddish legs. Might be confused with Red-necked Spurfowl but lacks bare red face and throat. **Habitat**: Woodland, especially riparian thickets. **Status**: Common. Usually found in pairs or small family groups, often foraging in the open in the early morning. **Voice**: Raucous screeching 'krr kik-ik-ik'. (Natalse fisant)

35 cm | Br: Jan–Dec

Orange River Francolin   E

Plumage varies greatly but is a paler version of Red-winged Francolin although it lacks the broad spangled breast band. Can be told apart from Grey-winged Francolin by having a white, not grey throat. Shelley's Francolin is similar but has black-barred, not buffy belly. **Habitat**: Grassland and semi-arid savanna. **Status**: Locally common. **Voice**: Rather strident 'kibitele', faster and higher-pitched than that of Shelley's Francolin, mostly at dawn. (Kalaharipatrys)

35 cm | Br: Sep–May

Grey-winged Francolin   E

Most diagnostic feature on this small, greyish francolin is its grey, not white or buffish speckled throat as in other similar francolins. In flight shows much less orange in the wings than other similar francolins. **Habitat**: Sand plain and mountain fynbos, S Karoo and montane grassland. **Status**: Fairly common to common; usually in coveys of 3–8 birds. **Voice**: Whistling, rather variable 'wip wip wip kipeeo, wip kipeeoo'. (Bergpatrys)

33 cm | Br: Aug–Mar

Red-winged Francolin   E

The black-flecked necklace, which forms a broad breast band, is the most diagnostic feature. The black freckling strongly contrasts with rich rufous collar and white throat. In flight shows a greater extent of orange on the wings than other similar francolins. **Habitat**: Grassland and fields in mountainous terrain, usually on lower slopes and in valleys. **Status**: Scarce to locally common; several populations have become rare due to unfavourable agricultural practices. **Voice**: Piping 'wip-tilleee', sometimes preceded by several short 'wip' notes. (Rooivlerkpatrys)

36–38 cm | Br: Jan–Dec   J F M A M J J A S O N D

Shelley's Francolin
The chestnut-blotched breast and strongly marked black-and-white barring on the lower breast and belly is diagnostic. The white throat is narrowly edged with black. **Habitat**: Savanna and open woodland, especially associated with rocky ground. **Status**: Locally common. **Voice**: Rhythmic, repeated 'til-it, til-leoo' ('I'll drink yer beer'); slower and less varied than other red-winged species. (Laeveldpatrys)

28–31 cm | Br: Aug–Jun | J F M A M J J A S O N D

Crested Francolin
A small, rotund game bird with a dark cap that contrasts with a broad white eyebrow stripe. The upperparts are reddish-brown streaked with buff, and the underparts show a dark freckled neck, throat and breast. Imm. is similar to ad. but has a buff eyebrow stripe. The tail is often held cocked, bantam-like, at an angle of 45°. **Habitat**: Woodland and well-wooded savanna. **Status**: Common. **Voice**: Rattling duet, 'chee-chakla, chee-chakla'. (Bospatrys)

33–35 cm | Br: Oct–May | J F M A M J J A S O N D

Coqui Francolin
Male of this small francolin is easily recognised by its uniform rusty-coloured head and neck, contrasting with black-barred breast. Female similar but much smaller than Shelley's Francolin but has broad white eyebrow stripe and lacks the chestnut striping on underparts. **Habitat**: Woodland and savanna, especially on sandy soils. **Status**: Common to locally common. **Voice**: Distinctive, disyllabic 'co-qui'; territorial 'ker-aak, aak, kara-kara-kara', with last notes fading away. (Swempie)

21–26 cm | Br: Jan–Dec | J F M A M J J A S O N D

Helmeted Guineafowl
Easily distinguishable by its rotund body and greyish plumage finely spotted with white. The naked blue and red head has red crown casque and wattles. Large groups sometimes form. When put to flight, they burst from cover and fly clumsily in follow-my-leader style before alighting some distance off. **Habitat**: Catholic; grassland, woodland, savanna and fields. **Status**: Common; may flock in hundreds. **Voice**: Loud 'kek kek kaaa, ke kaaa, ke kaaa'; monotonous, repeated 'krrdii-krrdii'; alarm note 'kek-kek-kek'. (Gewone tarentaal)

58–64 cm | Br: Sep–Mar | J F M A M J J A S O N D

Crested Guineafowl

A black game bird finely spotted with pale blue. The naked face is bluish-grey and the crown has a tuft of curly black feathers. In flight it shows a pale wing panel on the inner primaries. Often gathers in large flocks when not breeding. Roosts in trees, giving loud contact calls just before sunset. **Habitat**: Forest edge, thickets and dense woodland. **Status**: Locally common. **Voice**: 'Chik-chik-chil-urrrrr'; soft 'keet-keet-keet' contact call. (Kuifkoptarentaal)

46–51 cm | Br: Oct–Feb   J F M A M J J A S O N D

Common Buttonquail

Similar to, but smaller than Common Quail. It has a similar flight action to Common Quail but is faster and shows pale buffy patches in the wings. On the ground it runs rapidly or moves with slow, deliberate, chameleon-like steps when the pale eye would be visible. Female is more brightly coloured than male, with sex reversal role when the male incubates and raises the young. **Habitat**: Tall grassland, old fields and open savanna. **Status**: Locally common. **Voice**: Repeated, low-pitched hoot, 'hmmmm'. (Bosveldkwarteltjie)

14–15 cm | Br: Jan–Dec   J F M A M J J A S O N D

Harlequin Quail

Similar to Common Quail in size and flight action but has much darker, chestnut and black underparts. Shows a boldly patterned black-and-white throat and face markings. Female is darker than Common Quail. **Habitat**: Grassland, damp fields and savanna, often in moister areas than Common Quail. **Status**: Locally abundant nomad and intra-African migrant. **Voice**: High-pitched 'whit, wit-wit', more metallic than Common Quail's; squeaky 'kree-kree' in flight. (Bontkwartel)

14–15 cm | Br: Oct–Mar   J F M A M J J A S O N D

Common Quail

Most often seen when flushed. Small, rotund, buffy game bird with very rapid whirring wings. Swiftly runs through the grass, rodent-like with head hunched into body. Much paler than Harlequin Quail, lacking the dark underparts of that species. **Habitat**: Grassland, fields and croplands. **Status**: Locally abundant. **Voice**: Repeated, high-pitched 'whit wit-wit' ('wet my lips'), slower and deeper than Harlequin Quail's; shrill 'crwee-crwee' in flight. (Afrikaanse kwartel)

17–20 cm | Br: Sep–Mar   J F M A M J J A S O N D

Common Ostrich

Unmistakable: the tallest and largest bird in the region. Male has contrasting black-and-white plumage, a rufous tail, and a reddish front to the legs when breeding. Female and imm. are drab brown and white. Very young bird might be mistaken for a korhaan but has flattened bill, thick legs and is fluffy in appearance. **Habitat**: Open country, arid savanna and semi-desert plains. **Status**: Wild populations restricted to large reserves and wilderness areas; often farmed; feral birds widespread in S Africa. **Voice**: Booming, leonine roar, mostly at night. (Volstruis)

2 m | **Br:** Jan–Dec   J F M A M J J A S O N D   ♀ ♂

Secretarybird

Might be mistaken for a stork or crane when seen striding through the veld but the short, hooked bill, the black, partly feathered legs and the black, wispy nape plumes should rule out confusion. In flight it is almost vulture-like except that the central tail feathers are elongated and project well beyond the end of the tail, as do the long legs. Most frequently seen in pairs, hunting over open veld, stopping frequently to pick something from the ground. **Habitat**: Savanna and open grassland. **Status**: Uncommon to locally common. **Voice**: Normally silent. (Sekretarisvoël)

140 cm | **Br:** Jan–Dec   J F M A M J J A S O N D

Grey Crowned Crane

This large, long-legged bird is unmistakable. When in flight, the large white wing patches are conspicuous. Imm. lacks the bold white face patches of the ad. and has a less well-developed bristly golden crown. Has a diagnostic honking call in flight. Birds form large flocks when not breeding. Displaying birds dance around facing each other, holding their wings outstretched. **Habitat**: Shallow wetlands, grassland and agricultural lands; commutes to wetlands to roost. **Status**: Locally common. **Voice**: Trumpeting flight call, 'may hem'; deep 'huum huum' when breeding. (Mahem)

105–112 cm | **Br:** Oct–Jun   J F M A M J J A S O N D

Blue Crane   E

Overall impression is of a large, long-legged, greyish bird with a paler head and long, drooping tail. However, actual tail is very short and the drooping feathers are elongations of inner wing feathers. Feathers on breast are also elongated and sometimes give the bird a shaggy-breasted appearance. **Habitat**: Grassland and agricultural lands. **Status**: VULNERABLE. Locally common in SW, but decreasing in E grasslands. In small pairs or family groups while breeding, but non-br. flocks contain hundreds of birds. **Voice**: Loud, nasal 'kraaaank'. (Bloukraanvoël)

100 cm | **Br:** Aug–Apr   J F M A M J J A S O N D

Kori Bustard

Largest bustard in the region. Its large size, dark crest and lack of any rufous on the hind neck differentiate it from Denham's Bustard. In flight it further differs from that species by lacking white patches in the wing. Male is larger than juv. and female. Displaying male cocks tail and 'balloons' grey neck feathers. **Habitat**: Semi-arid savanna and grassland, usually near cover of trees. **Status**: Generally scarce, but locally fairly common in protected areas. **Voice**: Deep, resonant 'oom-oom-oom' by male during br. season. (Gompou)

105–135 cm | Br: Jul–Apr   J F M A M J J A S O N D

Denham's Bustard

Smaller than Kori Bustard. The pale grey foreneck and pale crown stripe are diagnostic in the male. In flight it shows extensive white patches in the wing. Displaying male puffs up white neck and breast feathers, which forms a conspicuous 'balloon'. Juv. and female smaller than male and have a more patterned back. **Habitat**: Open grassland and agricultural land. **Status**: Uncommon to locally common. **Voice**: Deep booming by displaying male. (Veldpou)

84–116 cm | Br: Sep–Dec   J F M A M J J A S O N D

Black-bellied Bustard

The back of both sexes is highly patterned with black and brown. Has an extremely long, thin neck and longish legs. Black underwings and belly extend to throat with a long, thin line on the foreneck. In flight shows striking and extensive white wing patches, which are diagnostic. Has a peculiar whistle and pop call and a strange, butterfly-like display flight. **Habitat**: Woodland and tall, open grassland. **Status**: Fairly common. **Voice**: Short, sharp 'chic' followed by a 'plop'. (Langbeenkorhaan)

58–63 cm | Br: Sep–Mar   J F M A M J J A S O N D

Karoo Korhaan   E

Plumage is variable but overall greyish-brown, lightly patterned back, plain unmarked face and a black throat patch. Female has less developed throat patch and both sexes in flight display buffy wing patches. **Habitat**: Karoo scrub; also croplands in S Cape. **Status**: Common; usually in groups of 2 or 3 birds. **Voice**: Deep, frog-like duet, 'wrok-rak' or 'wrok-rak-rak', mostly at dawn and dusk; male utters deeper first syllable, female responds. (Vaalkorhaan)

58 cm | Br: Jun–Feb   J F M A M J J A S O N D

Blue Korhaan E

The all-blue underparts on this korhaan are diagnostic and it is the only korhaan to show blue in the wings in flight. Sexes differ by male having a white face with a black ear patch whereas female has an unmarked face with a small white eyebrow stripe. **Habitat:** High elevation grassland and E Karoo. **Status:** Locally common; usually in small groups of 2–5 birds. **Voice:** Deep, discordant 'krok-ka-krow', generally at dawn and dusk. (Bloukorhaan)

56 cm | Br: May, Sep–Feb | J F M A M J J A S O N D

Red-crested Korhaan

Red crest is rarely visible except on a displaying male when a tuft of elongated, reddish feathers are erected and resemble in shape that of Grey Crowned Crane's crest. Courtship flight of male is when he bullets straight into the air and then plummets and tumbles to the ground. The black belly and underwings and white breast patches are diagnostic. **Habitat:** Dry woodland and semi-desert grassland. **Status:** Common; singly or in pairs. **Voice:** Song is protracted series of clicks. (Boskorhaan)

50 cm | Br: Sep–Mar | J F M A M J J A S O N D

Northern Black Korhaan E

Unmistakable, especially when male is seen in flight display during the br. season. The male, a striking black, white and barred brown bird, flies into the air and courses over its territory, calling continually. At the end of the display it slowly descends to the ground with slow-motion wing beats and its bright yellow legs dangling. Female is drabber and has the black restricted to the lower belly. **Habitat:** Karoo grassland and arid savannas. **Status:** Common; singly or in pairs. **Voice:** Male gives raucous 'kerrrak-kerrrak-kerrrak' in flight and on ground. (Witvlerkkorhaan)

52 cm | Br: Jul–Mar | J F M A M J J A S O N D

♀

Southern Black Korhaan E

Confusion with Northern Black Korhaan is unlikely due to their ranges not overlapping. Differs from that species in flight by lacking expansive white flashes in the primaries. Display flight has male flying randomly with dangling legs, giving its raucous call, ending in the bird parachuting to the ground. **Habitat:** Coastal fynbos and Karoo scrub. **Status:** Common; singly or in pairs. **Voice:** Male gives raucous 'kerrrak-kerrrak-kerrrak' in flight and on ground. (Swartvlerkkorhaan)

52 cm | Br: Aug–Jan | J F M A M J J A S O N D

Yellow-throated Sandgrouse

The largest sandgrouse in the region. Identified in flight by its short tail and dark brown belly and underwings. Male has a creamy yellow face and throat, with a broad black neck collar. Female is heavily mottled on the neck, breast and upperparts. **Habitat**: Grassland and arid savanna. **Status**: Locally common; drinks during the morning. **Voice**: Flight call a deep, far-carrying bi-syllabic 'aw-aw', the first higher pitched; sometimes preceded by 'ipi'. (Geelkeelsandpatrys)

28–30 cm | Br: Apr–Oct   J F M A M J J A S O N D

Double-banded Sandgrouse

Male differs from vaguely similar male Namaqua Sandgrouse by having black-and-white barring on the head. Female and juv. differ from female and juv. Namaqua Sandgrouse by having streaked crown and a rounded, not pointed tail. Congregates at water to drink at dusk. **Habitat**: Woodland and savanna, but also arid Karoo grassland in SW. **Status**: Locally common; drinks at dusk, often after dark. **Voice**: Whistling 'chwee-chee-chee' and soft 'wee-chee-choo-chip-chip' flight call. (Dubbelbandsandpatrys)

25–28 cm | Br: Feb–Oct   J F M A M J J A S O N D

Namaqua Sandgrouse   NE

A pigeon-sized bird and, in the region, the only sandgrouse with a long, pointed tail. In flight has very rapid wing beats and often gives its nasal 'kelkie-vein' call, which reveals its presence. Male has a buff-spotted back and a white and chestnut breast band; female is cryptically mottled and streaked with buff and brown but still shows the pointed tail. **Habitat**: Grassland, semi-desert and desert. **Status**: Common nomad and resident; drinks 1–4 hours after dawn. **Voice**: Flight call a nasal 'kelkie-vein'. (Kelkiewyn)

25 cm | Br: Jan–Dec   J F M A M J J A S O N D

Burchell's Sandgrouse   NE

The white-spotted cinnamon breast and belly, combined with the white-spotted back and wing coverts is diagnostic and render this small sandgrouse unmistakable. Male has a grey face with a yellow eye-ring. In flight shows diagnostic chestnut wing linings. **Habitat**: Semi-arid savanna; particularly common on Kalahari sands. **Status**: Scarce to locally common; drinks 3–5 hours after dawn, generally later in the day than Namaqua Sandgrouse. **Voice**: Flight call a soft, mellow 'chup-chup, choop-choop'. (Gevlekte sandpatrys)

25 cm | Br: Apr–Oct   J F M A M J J A S O N D

Bearded Vulture

The flight shape of this large bird of prey is diagnostic. It shows an outline of long slender wings, often held angled, a long slender body and a long wedge-shaped tail. The tail is usually held closed and appears pointed. The orange underparts contrast with the dark underwings and only at close range can the bristles on the chin be seen which gives the bird its name. Imm. is overall darker but still has the characteristic shape of the adult. **Habitat:** The Drakensberg and Maluti mountains. **Status:** Uncommon. **Voice:** Usually silent. (Baardaasvoël)

110 cm | Br: May–Aug   J F M A M J J A S O N D

Lappet-faced Vulture

The bare red skin on the face and throat are diagnostic in the ad. When seen flying overhead the white thighs and white stripe running across the forepart of the underwing are clearly visible diagnostic features. Juv. and imm. lack the white thighs and underwing but are very much darker than juv. White-backed and Cape vultures. **Habitat:** Savanna, especially in more arid areas; nests and roosts on trees. **Status:** VULNERABLE. Locally fairly common. Solitary or in loose colonies. **Voice:** High-pitched whistling display. (Swartaasvoël)

78–115 cm | Br: May–Oct   J F M A M J J A S O N D

White-headed Vulture

This small vulture is the only one in the region to have a white head, black breast and contrasting white underparts. In flight female shows large white secondary patches; male's are correspondingly dark and contrast with white belly. Juv. is all dark. **Habitat:** Open savanna; roosts and nests on trees. **Status:** Uncommon to locally common; solitary; pairs sedentary and may be territorial. **Voice:** High-pitched chittering. (Witkopaasvoël)

78–84 cm | Br: May–Oct   J F M A M J J A S O N D

Cape Vulture   E

Very similar to White-backed Vulture but this species is very much larger and is paler overall. If seen from above the lack of white lower back eliminates confusion and, when seen close by, the eye is honey-coloured, not dark; also shows two naked blue patches on sides of breast. **Habitat:** Grassland and arid savanna; scarce in well-wooded savanna; roosts and nests on cliffs. **Status:** VULNERABLE. Range has contracted, but remains locally common in core of range. **Voice:** Cackling and hissing. (Kransaasvoël)

100–115 cm | Br: Apr–Jul   J F M A M J J A S O N D

White-backed Vulture

The common vulture of bushveld game reserves. If seen when the bird is banking in flight or holding its wings outstretched, the white lower back contrasts with the darker wings (diagnostic). Imm. is very much darker than ad. and shows less contrast between flight feathers and wing linings. Most often seen in flight, either riding the thermals or high in the air searching the ground for kills. **Habitat**: Savanna and open woodland. **Status**: Common; usually most abundant vulture away from human habitation. **Voice**: Harsh cackles and hisses. (Witrugaasvoël)

95 cm | Br: Apr–Sep   J F M A M J J A S O N D

African Fish Eagle

Easily identified by the combination of white head and breast, dark body, chestnut forewings and white tail. Imm. is difficult to distinguish from other brown eagles but it shows a relatively short tail and a shadow image of ad.'s white breast. **Habitat**: Large rivers, lakes, estuaries and lagoons; occasionally hunts close inshore over sea. **Status**: Common. **Voice**: Ringing 'kyow-kow-kow' with head thrown back, from perches or in flight; male's call is higher pitched. (Visarend)

63–73 cm | Br: Mar–Aug   J F M A M J J A S O N D

Bateleur

Easily identified because of its unusual shape in flight: appears to have virtually no tail and has very contrasting black-and-white underwings. The wing shape is also unusual, being narrow at the body and tips and broadening towards the centre. Male has a much broader black trailing edge to the wing than female. Imm. is a brown version of ad. Flight is direct on slightly canted wings and bird careens from side to side. **Habitat**: Savanna. Found over open thornveld in major game reserves. **Status**: Uncommon. **Voice**: Loud bark, 'kow-wah'. (Berghaan)

55–70 cm | Br: Jan–May   J F M A M J J A S O N D

Brown Snake Eagle

A smallish brown eagle best distinguished from other small brown eagles by its unfeathered, creamy-white legs. Appears to have an unusually large, rounded head with bright golden-yellow eyes. In flight the dark brown wing linings contrast strongly with silvery white flight feathers. **Habitat**: Savanna and woodland. **Status**: Locally common; nomadic. **Voice**: Croaking 'hok-hok-hok-hok' flight call; generally silent. (Bruinslangarend)

66–71 cm | Br: Jul–Aug, Nov–Mar   J F M A M J J A S O N D

Black-chested Snake Eagle

Medium-sized eagle that displays diagnostic large, rounded, dark head with bright yellow eyes. In flight the underwing is pale and finely barred, contrasting with the black breast. Imm. very different from ad. and is overall rich brown, with barring on wings and tail. Shows same large head shape as ad. **Habitat**: Ranges from desert to savanna and woodland. **Status**: Uncommon to locally common nomad and possible intra-African migrant. **Voice**: Rarely calls; melodious, whistled 'kwo-kwo-kwo-kweeu'. (Swartborsslangarend)

63 60 cm | Br: Mar–Oct   J F M A M J J A S O N D

Tawny Eagle

A large eagle, very variable in colour, from dark brown to pale buff, depending on age. Differs from smaller Wahlberg's Eagle by its broader tail and wings. Ad. has a pale yellow eye. Female is a darker brown and juv. is dark brown, fading to buff as it ages. Sometimes gathers in flocks to forage on termite emergences, when they waddle around in ungainly fashion while picking up the insects off the ground. **Habitat**: Savanna and woodland. **Status**: Common resident and local migrant. **Voice**: Seldom calls; sharp bark, 'kyow'. (Roofarend)

66–73 cm | Br: Mar–Sep   J F M A M J J A S O N D

Verreaux's Eagle

This large black-and-white eagle is unmistakable. From above shows white edging to scapulars and a conspicuous white rump. From below it appears all black with large white-barred patches in the primaries. Juv. is variegated brown with a pale rufous buff crown and nape, and white patches in the primaries. Feeds mainly on rock hyrax, but is also known to scavenge at carcasses. **Habitat**: Mountainous areas. **Status**: Locally common. **Voice**: Rarely calls; melodious 'keee-uup'. (Witkruisarend)

82–96 cm | Br: Apr–Jul   J F M A M J J A S O N D

Crowned Eagle

Ad. is dark grey above, rufous below with breast and belly heavily barred and mottled with black. In flight has a long tail, rounded wings and heavily barred underwings with rufous wing linings. Its large size and hawk-like appearance in flight make this a distinctive eagle. Juv. is white below. **Habitat**: Forest and dense woodland. **Status**: Locally fairly common. **Voice**: Very vocal; flight call is ringing 'kewee-kewee-kewee'; male's call is higher pitched. (Kroonarend)

82–92 cm | Br: Jun–Mar   J F M A M J J A S O N D

Long-crested Eagle

This small, dark brown eagle is instantly recognisable by its long, wispy crest and white-feathered legs. In flight it shows distinct white 'windows' in the wings and its barred black-and-white tail. When not soaring, the flight action is swift and direct with shallow wing beats. May be seen perched on dead trees or telephone poles. **Habitat**: Woodland, plantations and forest edges, especially near water. **Status**: Common resident and local nomad. **Voice**: High-pitched, screamed 'kee-ah' during display or when perched. (Langkuifarend)

52–58 cm | Br: Jul–Jan | J F M A M J J A S O N D

Booted Eagle

A small buzzard-sized eagle with both dark and light forms. Could be confused with Wahlberg's Eagle but differs by having broader, shorter tail and broader wings. The pale form has finely spotted white wing linings and head appears hooded. Small white patches to the base of the forewing, known as braces, are diagnostic for both forms. **Habitat**: Virtually any habitat, but avoids extensive forests; breeds on cliffs. **Status**: Uncommon; breeds in extreme SW; Palaearctic and intra-African migrant. **Voice**: High-pitched 'kee-keeee' or 'pee-pee-pee-pee'. (Dwergarend)

48–51 cm | Br: Aug–Dec | J F M A M J J A S O N D

Wahlberg's Eagle

A medium-sized eagle which is very variable in colour, from buffy to all dark brown (commonest form), white head and underparts to rufous with a dark head. Flight shape is stiffly held straight wings and long, square-ended narrow tail. At rest shows a short, pointed crest. **Habitat**: Woodland and savanna. **Status**: Common intra-African migrant. **Voice**: Drawn-out whistle while soaring; yelping 'kop-yop-yip-yip-yip' when perched. (Bruinarend)

55–60 cm | Br: Aug–Dec | J F M A M J J A S O N D

Augur Buzzard

Similar in shape and overall structure to Jackal Buzzard but differs in having white throat, breast and belly and white, not dark lining to the underwings. Some Jackal Buzzards show white breasts but their underwing linings all remain dark, not white. Juv. is a browner version of ad. and hardly distinguishable in the field from juv. Jackal Buzzard except that their ranges don't overlap. **Habitat**: Mountain ranges and hilly country in woodland, savanna and desert. **Status**: Common. **Voice**: Harsh 'kow-kow-kow-kow' display call. (Witborsjakkalsvoël)

55–60 cm | Br: Jul–Nov | J F M A M J J A S O N D

Jackal Buzzard   E

Larger than Steppe Buzzard and not as variable in plumage coloration. When perched appears very dark above, with a bright chestnut breast and barred black-and-white belly. In flight the combination of contrasting black-and-white underwings and bright chestnut breast and tail is diagnostic. Imm. has rufous-brown underparts and a comparatively pale tail. **Habitat**: Karoo scrub, grassland and agricultural lands; usually breeds on cliffs. **Status**: Locally common. **Voice**: Loud, drawn-out 'weeaah-ka-ka-ka'; male's call is higher pitched. (Rooiborsjakkalsvoël)

55–60 cm | Br: Jun–Feb   J F M A M **J J A** S O N D

Steppe Buzzard

Not readily distinguishable from many similar raptors in the region but most individuals show a pale, broad crescent across the breast. Colours range from almost pale buff to dark brown or black, but the breast pattern is fairly constant. Present only during summer and then very common, being the most abundant medium-sized raptor seen perched on telephone poles. Flight is strong and direct except when soaring or gliding. **Habitat**: Open country, avoiding very arid and forested areas. **Status**: Abundant Palaearctic migrant. **Voice**: Seldom calls in Africa. (Bruinjakkalsvoël)

45–50 cm | Br: n/a   J F M A M J J A S O N D

African Harrier-Hawk

Might be confused with chanting goshawks but has much broader, more floppy wings and has distinctive single white bar on the tail. At close range the bare facial skin can appear yellow or red. Juv. and imm. can appear barred dark and grey but floppy flight on its broad wings helps identify it. **Habitat**: Woodland and forests; also more open, scrubby habitats. **Status**: Fairly common. **Voice**: During br. season, whistled 'suuu-eeee-ooo'. (Kaalwangvalk)

60–66 cm | Br: Aug–Nov   J F M A M J J A S O N D

African Marsh-Harrier

Differs from Yellow-billed Kite by having a long, thin, square, not forked tail and by its flight mode, which is direct on angled wings. Differs from brownish Steppe Buzzard by its longer, thinner tail and narrower wings and flight mode. Juv. has a creamy top to head and throat. **Habitat**: Marshes, reed beds and adjacent grassland. **Status**: Locally common to scarce. **Voice**: Mainly silent; display call high-pitched 'fee-ooo'. (Afrikaanse vleivalk)

45–50 cm | Br: Jul–Dec   J F M A M **J J A S O N D**

Black Harrier E

Unmistakable pied, black-and-white raptor. At rest appears all sooty-black but in flight shows white-barred underwings and a white rump. Juv. more slender than African Marsh-Harrier, with narrower wings and showing a white rump in flight. **Habitat**: Grassland and scrub, often near water, but forages over dry land. **Status**: VULNERABLE. Uncommon resident in SW, nomadic elsewhere. **Voice**: Generally silent; 'pee-pee-pee-pee' display call; harsh 'chak-chak-chak' when alarmed. (Witkruisvleivalk)

48–53 cm | Br: Jun–Nov | J F M A M J J A S O N D

Pale Chanting Goshawk NE

Larger than either the African or Gabar goshawks and has longer legs. Habitually rests on exposed perches from which it hunts. When put to flight, its upperparts show a white rump and white trailing edges to the wings and secondaries, which contrast with the darker primaries. Imm. is dark brown above and streaked and blotched with brown below. **Habitat**: Semi-arid areas. **Status**: Common; three adults often breed together. **Voice**: A piping 'kleeu-kleeu-klu-klu-klu'. (Bleeksingvalk)

48–63 cm | Br: Mar–Dec | J F M A M J J A S O N D

Dark Chanting Goshawk

Can be confused with Southern Pale Chanting Goshawk but is overall darker grey. Most obvious difference is that the wings in this bird do not have white secondaries and at rest show less contrast, being more uniform. Juv. differs by having a darker brown breast and a barred brown, not white rump. **Habitat**: Savanna and open woodland. **Status**: Uncommon; less obtrusive than other chanting goshawks. **Voice**: Piping 'kleeu-kleeu-klu-klu-klu'. (Donkersingvalk)

43–56 cm | Br: Jul–Nov | J F M A M J J A S O N D

Yellow-billed Kite

The kite seen patrolling roads and frequenting towns and cities. In ad. plumage the yellow bill and cere are diagnostic. This large bird of prey is readily distinguished from others by its forked tail, which it twists in flight from the horizontal to the almost vertical as it steers and manoeuvres through the air. Imm. is darker and has a black, not yellow bill. **Habitat**: Woodland and open habitats; this is the kite commonly seen around human habitation. **Status**: Common intra-African migrant. **Voice**: Call is a whinnying 'kleeeuw' trill. (Geelbekwou)

51–60 cm | Br: Aug–Dec | J F M A M J J A S O N D

Black-shouldered Kite

A small, conspicuous bird of prey that is commonly seen sitting on telephone wires and poles, or hovering over the veld or road verges. Ad. is grey and white with a diagnostic black shoulder patch and deep, cherry-red eye. When perched it occasionally flicks its short white tail. When stooping for food, its wings are held over its back like a parachute. Imm. is dowdier than ad. and has a buff and brown-barred back. **Habitat**: Savanna, grassland and agricultural areas. **Status**: Common. **Voice**: High-pitched, whistled 'peeeu'; soft 'weep'; rasping 'wee-ah'. (Blouvalk)

33 cm | **Br:** Jan–Dec | J F M A M J J A S O N D

Lizard Buzzard

Can be confused with Gabar Goshawk but is broader and bulkier in shape and has a diagnostic black line down its white throat. In flight shows a conspicuous white rump and a single, rarely two, white tail bar(s). Juv. similar to ad. but has a paler base to bill and darker eyes. **Habitat**: Woodland, well-wooded savanna and forest clearings. **Status**: Locally common resident; nomadic in drier areas. **Voice**: Noisy in br. season: whistled 'peoo-peoo'; melodious 'klioo-klu-klu-klu-klu'. (Akkedisvalk)

35–37 cm | **Br:** May–Jan | J F M A M J J A S O N D

Pygmy Falcon

This tiny raptor could be mistaken for a shrike. It sits on exposed perches from where it hunts. Male has a grey back, female has chestnut back. Juv. resembles female but has dull brown back and underparts washed with rufous. Very often associated with Sociable Weaver's nests. **Habitat**: Arid savanna. Breeds in nests of Sociable Weavers and buffalo-weavers, leaving distinctive, white-washed rim around nest entrance. **Status**: Uncommon to locally common. **Voice**: Noisy; high-pitched 'chip-chip' and 'kik-kik-kik-kik'. (Dwergvalk)

18–20 cm | **Br:** Aug–Mar | J F M A M J J A S O N D   ♂ ♀

Gabar Goshawk

Superficially resembles the African Goshawk but has a grey throat and breast, red, not yellow eyes, cere and legs and a white, not dark rump. Imm. differs markedly, having a rufous-streaked and mottled head and breast, but it still shows a white rump. A very bold and conspicuous goshawk that regularly sits on exposed perches. An uncommon black form occurs, which can be identified by its red cere and legs. **Habitat**: Savanna and semi-arid scrub with at least some trees. **Status**: Locally common. **Voice**: High-pitched, whistling 'kik-kik-kik-kik-kik'. (Witkruissperwer)

28–36 cm | **Br:** Mar Jul–Dec | J F M A M J J A S O N D

Shikra

Differs from Little Sparrowhawk by lacking white rump and tail spots and from Gabar Goshawk by lacking white rump and having a bright cherry-red eye if seen close up. Juv. differs from very similar Gabar Goshawk by lacking a white rump. Usually solitary but more visual than other small hawks; frequently seen spiralling over wooded areas. **Habitat**: Savanna and tall woodland. **Status**: Common resident and local nomad. **Voice**: Male high-pitched 'keewik-keewik-keewik'; female softer 'kee-uuu'. (Gebande sperwer)

28–30 cm | **Br:** Aug–Feb | J F M A M J J A S O N D

Little Sparrowhawk

This tiny hawk is most easily confused with the larger Shikra but can be told apart by its white rump and large white upper-tail spots. Also closely resembles African Goshawk but is very much smaller and has the tail spots and white rump. **Habitat**: Forest, woodland and plantations. **Status**: Locally common but secretive. **Voice**: Male a high-pitched 'tu tu tu tu' when breeding; female a softer 'kew kew kew'. (Kleinsperwer)

23–28 cm | **Br:** Sep–Dec | J F M A M J J A S O N D

Black Sparrowhawk

This bird's large size and pied, black-and-white plumage render it unmistakable. A rare all-black form occurs and could be confused with dark form Gabar Goshawk but is immensely larger. Imm. has a brown-streaked plumage and resembles many other brown-streaked raptors but its yellow, naked legs and sparrowhawk flight action should help to identify it. **Habitat**: Forests, woodland and plantations; sometimes forages far from cover. **Status**: Locally fairly common. **Voice**: Normally silent except when breeding. Male 'kee-yip'; female loud 'kek-kek-kek-kek'. (Swartsperwer)

46–58 cm | **Br:** Mar–Dec | J F M A M J J A S O N D

Rufous-chested Sparrowhawk

Ad. is easily identified by having uniform rufous underparts, slate greyish upperparts and the lack of a white rump. Female is very much larger than male but they have the same coloration. Imm. similar to ad. but is more mottled brown and rufous on the underparts. **Habitat**: Montane forest patches and plantations; often forages far from cover. **Status**: Locally common. **Voice**: Sharp, staccato 'kee-kee-kee-kee-kee' during display. (Rooiborssperwer)

25–28 cm | **Br:** Aug–Dec | J F M A M J J A S O N D

African Goshawk

Combination of blue-grey head and dark back with pale underparts finely barred with reddish, helps distinguish ad. Male is smaller than female, and brighter. Imm. has reddish barring on underparts replaced with large, drop-shaped dark brown spots, and shows a dark line down the white throat. Seen most often during early morning display when it flies high over its territory, giving a short 'whit' call every few seconds. **Habitat**: Forest and dense woodland. **Status**: Common. **Voice**: Noisy; repetitive 'whit' or 'quick'. (Afrikaanse sperwer)

36 46 cm | **Br**: Jul–Dec   J F M A M J J A S O N D

Lanner Falcon

A medium-sized falcon, the ad. of which shows a rufous crown and an unmarked pinkish breast. Imm. has a buffy streaked crown and heavily streaked underparts. In flight this species shows wings that are relatively broad at the base, and which narrow into points. Flight is slow and floppy compared to that of smaller falcons; however, it is rapid when chasing prey; executes fast-angled stoops to strike prey in mid-air. **Habitat**: Occurs in a wide range of habitats, from mountains and deserts to open grasslands. **Status**: Common. **Voice**: A harsh 'kak-kak'. (Edelvalk)

38–45 cm | **Br**: May–Sep   J F M A M J J A S O N D

Peregrine Falcon

Confused with Lanner Falcon, from which it is easily distinguished by its lack of a pale crown and having finely barred, not creamy spotted underparts. Juv. differs from juv. Lanner by its pale, not dark grey crown and nape. Flight action more dynamic than Lanner with rapid wing beats and very swift stoops at prey on the wing. **Habitat**: Migrant birds occur in a wide range of habitats but forage regularly over wetlands. Resident birds require high cliffs and gorges. **Status**: Uncommon resident and migrant. **Voice**: Raucous 'kak kak kak kak' around breeding sites. (Swerfvalk)

34–38 cm | **Br**: Jul–Nov   J F M A M J J A S O N D

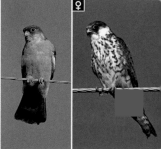

Amur Falcon

A small falcon whose overall dark grey plumage is relieved only by contrasting white wing linings and a chestnut vent. Cere, legs and feet are bright red, a feature that can be seen at close range. Female has a pale greyish head with black moustachial stripes, grey upperparts, pale underparts heavily streaked with black, a chestnut vent, and red legs and feet. Imm. similar to female but has finer streaking below. **Habitat**: Open grassland. Roosts communally in tall trees. **Status**: Common Palaearctic migrant. **Voice**: Shrill chattering at roosts. (Oostelike rooipootvalk)

30 cm | **Br**: n/a   J F M A M J J A S O N D

Red-footed Falcon

Confusable only with Amur Falcon from which it differs in having dark, not white wing linings. Female has deep buffy underparts and head with a dark eye patch. Juv. is similar to female but with paler head and heavily streaked underparts; might be confused with Eurasian Hobby but has paler head and much paler underparts and lacks rufous vent. **Habitat**: Grassland and arid savanna. Roosts communally in tall trees. **Status**: Fairly common Palaearctic migrant, mostly Oct–Apr. **Voice**: Shrill chattering at roosts. (Westelike rooipootvalk)

29–31 cm | **Br:** n/a   J F M A M J J A S O N D

Lesser Kestrel

Slightly smaller than Rock Kestrel. Male distinguished from Rock Kestrel by having a uniform chestnut back and a blue band across the secondaries of upperwing. White toenails are diagnostic but are apparent only at close range. Female and imm. closely resemble female and imm. Rock Kestrel but, in summer, the Lesser Kestrel tends to form large flocks to feed and roost. **Habitat**: Arid shrubland, grassland and fields. Roosts communally in tall trees. **Status**: VULNERABLE. Locally abundant Palaearctic migrant. **Voice**: Silent during day, but noisy at roosts. (Kleinrooivalk)

29–33 cm | **Br:** n/a   J F M A M J J A S O N D

Rock Kestrel

Similar to Lesser Kestrel but male has a spotted, not uniform chestnut back, and lacks blue on his secondaries. Female difficult to distinguish from female Lesser Kestrel but Lesser has tendency to form flocks which this species does not do. Imm. lacks blue-grey on the head and tail. When hunting it hovers into the wind, remaining stationary with only its wings moving and tail spread before dropping swiftly onto its prey. **Habitat**: Grassland, scrub and open woodland. Breeds on cliffs or buildings. **Status**: Common. **Voice**: High-pitched 'kik-ki-ki'. (Kransvalk)

30–33 cm | **Br:** Jul–Jan   J F M A M J J A S O N D

Greater Kestrel

If seen close up, the pale eye is diagnostic and it is the only falcon in the region to show this. Differs from Rock Kestrel by being larger, with broader wings and a distinctive whitish underwing. Much larger than similar Lesser Kestrel but has a grey barred tail and lacks moustachial stripes. **Habitat**: Arid savanna and semi-desert. **Status**: Locally common. **Voice**: Shrill, repeated 'kee-ker-rik'. (Grootrooivalk)

36–40 cm | **Br:** Mar–Jan   J F M A M J J A S O N D

Verreaux's Eagle-Owl

This is the largest owl in the region and its huge size, overall greyish colour, dark eyes and pinkish eyelids are diagnostic. Juv. is a much paler grey than ad. and is very finely barred on the underparts. Its huge size makes this owl very easily seen on its daytime roosts. **Habitat**: Broad-leaved woodland, savanna, thornveld and riverine forests. **Status**: Uncommon to locally common resident. **Voice**: Grunting, pig-like 'unnh-unnh-unnh'. (Reuse-ooruil)

58–66 cm | Br: May–Sep   J F M A M J J A S O N D

Spotted Eagle-Owl

The commonest eagle-owl of the region. Occurs in a grey and rufous form, the greyish form being the commonest. Eye colour is a bright yellow in the grey form and more orange in the rare rufous form. Often seen on roads at night when picking up small roadkill, very often ending up as roadkill itself. **Habitat**: All except forest, from desert to woodland and gardens. **Status**: Common. **Voice**: Male gives deep 'hoo-huuu', often followed by female's 'huu-ho huuu', with second note higher pitched. (Gevlekte ooruil)

43–50 cm | Br: Jan–Dec   J F M A M J J A S O N D

Western Barn Owl

Active at dusk or dawn, this owl appears very pale and is silent on the wing. At rest during the day, the white, heart-shaped face with black eyes, and faintly spotted, light buffy underparts with richer golden upperparts identify this owl. When startled during the day, it moves from side to side while peering at the intruder. **Habitat**: Open habitats, from woodland to desert; avoids dense forest. Often roosts in old buildings, but also in caves, hollow trees and mine shafts; doesn't roost on ground. **Status**: Common. **Voice**: Typical call is high-pitched 'shreeee'. (Nonnetjie-uil)

33–36 cm | Br: Jan–Dec   J F M A M J J A S O N D

African Wood Owl

A medium-sized owl with a rounded head lacking ear tufts, dark, not yellow eyes and a yellow bill. The pale facial disc contrasts with the white-spotted dark head and dark breast. The underparts are heavily barred dark brown and the overall plumage can be variable, ranging from very dark brown to russet. **Habitat**: Evergreen and riverine forests, mature woodland and alien plantations. **Status**: Common. **Voice**: Female calls 'hu hu, hu whoo-oo', with male normally responding with low hoot; also gives high-pitched 'who-uuu'. (Bosuil)

33–35 cm | Br: Jul–Nov   J F M A M J J A S O N D

Marsh Owl

A medium-sized owl of open areas. Plain brown with a greyish-buff face, small ear tufts and dark brown eyes. In flight shows buff panels on the primaries with dark carpal patches on the underwing. When flushed during the day it invariably circles around overhead before alighting. **Habitat**: Marshes and damp grassland. Sometimes roosts in flocks. **Status**: Common. **Voice**: Harsh, rasping 'krikkk-krikkk', like material being torn. (Vlei-uil)

35 cm | **Br: Jan–Dec** | J F M A M J J A S O N D

Southern White-faced Owl

This and the African Scops-Owl are the only two small owls with ear tufts. Confusion between the two is hardly likely because this species has a large white facial disc, is overall much paler grey, is very much larger and has bright orange, not yellow eyes. Juv. is a buffer version of ad. **Habitat**: Acacia savanna and dry, broad-leaved woodland. **Status**: Common. **Voice**: A fast, hooting 'doo-doo-doo-doo-hohoo'. (Witwanguil)

25–28 cm | **Br: Feb, May–Nov** | J F M A M J J A S O N D

African Barred Owlet

Really only confusable with Pearl-spotted Owlet from which it differs chiefly by having a very obviously barred head, underparts and tail and being noticeably larger. On the upperparts it shows conspicuous white edgings to the scapular feathers. **Habitat**: Mature woodland, thickets and forest edge. **Status**: Locally common. **Voice**: Series of 6–10 notes, starting softly and increasing in volume 'kerrr kerrr kerrr', often followed by a series of soft, purring whistles 'trru-trree', the second note being higher. (Gebande uil)

20–21 cm | **Br: May, Aug–Nov** | J F M A M J J A S O N D

Pearl-spotted Owlet

Easily told from African and Southern White-faced scops-owls by having a rounded head, lacking ear tufts and having conspicuous white spotting on the back and tail. Differentiated from African Barred Owlet by its smaller size and lacking barring on the head and underparts. It shows two black 'false eyes' on the nape. **Habitat**: Acacia savanna and dry woodland. **Status**: Common. **Voice**: Series of low hoots, rising in pitch, 'tu tu tu tu tu', then a brief pause followed by a series of piercing, down-slurred whistles, 'tseeu tseeu tseeu'. (Witkoluil)

18–19 cm | **Br: Aug–Nov** | J F M A M J J A S O N D

African Scops Owl

The smallest owl in the region that might be confused with the small Pearl-spotted Owl but has conspicuous ear tufts. Occurs in a grey and brown form and very cryptically coloured; very difficult to detect in their daytime roosts. They compress their bodies and sit tight against the tree trunk where they remain motionless and virtually invisible for hours. **Habltat**: Savanna and dry, open woodland; avoids forests. Typically roosts on branch adjacent to tree trunk. **Status**: Common. **Voice**: Soft, frog-like 'prrrup', repeated every 5–8 seconds. (Skopsuil)

15 17 cm | **Br:** Jun–Nov   J F M A M J J A S O N D

Freckled Nightjar

Larger than both Fiery-necked and Rufous-cheeked nightjars and is overall much darker. The greyish mottled and flecked upperparts camouflage the bird well in the rocky terrain it frequents. Often seen flying and calling just before sunset in the half-light of dusk. Usually solitary or in pairs. **Habitat**: Rocky outcrops in woodland and hilly terrain; also found roosting on buildings in towns and cities. **Status**: Locally common. **Voice**: Yapping, double-noted 'kow-kow', sometimes extending to four syllables. (Donkernaguil)

23–26 cm | **Br:** Aug–Dec   J F M A M J J A S O N D

Fiery-necked Nightjar

Nightjars are nocturnal and are very difficult to observe; even if flushed during the day, identification depends on a few seconds' view before the bird vanishes. The features to look for in the male are the white markings on the tail and wings, and in the female the white outer-tail spots which differentiate it from similar nightjars. **Habitat**: Woodland, savanna and plantations. **Status**: Common. **Voice**: Characteristic night sound of Africa: plaintive, whistled 'good lord, deliver us', descending in pitch, first note often repeated. (Afrikaanse naguil)

22–24 cm | **Br:** Aug–Dec   J F M A M J J A S O N D

Rufous-cheeked Nightjar

Very similar to Fiery-necked Nightjar but differs by having an orange-buff collar, not rufous and in lacking a rufous breast. Female very difficult to tell apart from female Fiery-necked Nightjar but generally shows a lot less buff in the tail and a smaller buff patch on the primaries. **Habitat**: Dry thornveld, woodland and scrub desert. **Status**: Locally common intra-African migrant, breeding in S mostly Oct–Apr. **Voice**: Prolonged churring, usually preceded by choking 'chukoo, chukoo'. (Rooiwangnaguil)

24 cm | **Br:** Aug–Jan   J F M A M J J A S O N D

Speckled Pigeon

Appears very dark in the field but, at close range, the finely white-speckled reddish back and wings and the bare red skin around the eyes are diagnostic. **Habitat**: Rocky areas, coastal cliffs and cities, ranging into fields and grassland to feed. **Status**: Common. Occurs in flocks, and is sometimes found in substantial numbers over stubble cornfields; has adapted to urban life and is frequently seen on ledges of buildings. **Voice**: Deep, booming 'hooo-hooo-hooo'. (Kransduif)

30–34 cm | Br: Jan–Dec   J F M A M J J A S O N D

African Olive Pigeon

By far the largest dove or pigeon in the region and appears the darkest of all. Only in bright sunlight or at close range can the bright yellow bill, bare skin around the eyes and on the legs and feet be seen. The plumage is a mixture of dark maroons, grey and blue, finely speckled with white. In flight the bird appears almost black but the sun often highlights the yellow bill or feet. **Habitat**: Forest, thickets and plantations. **Status**: Common. **Voice**: Low, raucous 'coo'. (Geelbekbosduif)

37–42 cm | Br: Jan–Dec   J F M A M J J A S O N D

African Green Pigeon

This pigeon is unmistakable with its bright green, grey and yellow plumage with a chestnut vent. When feeding it clambers about, parrot-like, often hanging upside down on branches to obtain fruit. In flight shows a broad white tip to undertail. **Habitat**: Forest, woodland and savanna; always associated with fruiting trees. **Status**: Common; subject to local movements. **Voice**: Distinctive series of un-pigeon-like croaks, wails and whinnying. (Papegaaiduif)

25–28 cm | Br: Jan–Dec   J F M A M J J A S O N D

Rock Dove

This is the common street pigeon familiar to anyone who lives in a city. It occurs in a variety of plumages: the most common colour combination is a dark grey body, an iridescent sheen on the neck, a white rump and pale grey wings which show two black bars. **Habitat**: Mostly in urban areas. Away from cities, it is often seen in the vicinity of farmsteads or in flocks of racing pigeons winging across the veld. **Status**: Common in many urban areas. **Voice**: Deep, rolling 'coo-roo-coo'. (Tuinduif)

33 cm | Br: Jan–Dec   J F M A M J J A S O N D

Red-eyed Dove

The largest and darkest of the 'ring-neck' doves. The eye and the bare skin surrounding it are red – a feature normally seen only at close range. Unlike the Cape Turtle-Dove it shows no white in the tail but it does have a grey band on the undertail and a diagnostic black band at the base of the tail. Imm. is very similar to ad. but has a reduced ring on the neck. **Habitat**: Woodland, forest and gardens. **Status**: Common. **Voice**: Typical call, 'coo coo', is diagnostic; harsh 'chwaa' alarm call. (Grootringduif)

30–33 cm | Br: Jan–Dec   J F M A M J J A S O N D

Cape Turtle Dove

The 'ring-neck' dove that shows a diagnostic white tip and sides to the tail in flight. This dove is much paler and smaller than the Red-eyed Dove, which lacks white in the tail. Probably the most abundant dove in the region. Display flight consists of the bird flying up at a low angle and then descending slowly with wings and tail spread. **Habitat**: Almost all, except forest. **Status**: Abundant. **Voice**: Well-known 'kuk-coorrrr-uk' ('how's father?'), middle note descending and trilled; harsh 'kurrrr' alarm call. (Gewone tortelduif)

25–28 cm | Br: Jan–Dec   J F M A M J J A S O N D

Laughing Dove

Smaller than Cape Turtle-Dove and lacks the black hind collar of that species. It has a pinkish-grey body, pale blue forewings and a finely black-speckled breast. In flight lacks the white tail tip seen in the Cape Turtle-Dove but has conspicuous white outer-tail feathers. The call, from which it derives its name, is a chortled cooing. **Habitat**: Wide range; not present in arid areas but inhabits a wide range of bush and farmlands and occurs in many towns and cities. **Status**: Common. **Voice**: Distinctive rising and falling 'uh huh u huu hu'. (Rooiborsduifie)

22–24 cm | Br: Jan–Dec   J F M A M J J A S O N D

Emerald-spotted Wood Dove

A small dove that is often seen in game reserves when it is flushed from roadsides or congregates at waterholes. In flight it shows reddish wing patches and two black bars on its rump; it is only at close range and in sunlight that the green wing spots can be seen. **Habitat**: Found in thornveld and dry, broad-leaved woodland. **Status**: Common. **Voice**: The characteristic call is a series of descending 'du-du' notes. (Groenvlekduifie)

16–20 cm | Br: Jan–Dec   J F M A M J J A S O N D

Tambourine Dove
An easily recognised small forest dove with its white face and underparts. Its flight is swift and dashing when the chestnut wing patches contrast strongly with the white body plumage. Female and juv. have duskier underparts but are still much paler below than any other small dove. **Habitat**: Forest, secondary forest, thickets and tropical plantations; feeds on the ground. **Status**: Common. **Voice**: Series of 'du du du du' notes, similar to other wood-doves but not changing in intensity at the end. (Witborsduifie)

20–22 cm | **Br:** Sep–Mar   J F M A M J J A S O N D

Namaqua Dove
A small-bodied dove that has a long, pointed tail, and a black face and throat. In flight the combination of the long, pointed tail, pale underparts and chestnut flight feathers render this bird unmistakable. Shows iridescent blue spots on the wings. Imm. and female lack the black face of male but show a shorter pointed tail and chestnut flight feathers. **Habitat**: Prefers drier regions such as thornveld, scrub and semi-desert. **Status**: Locally common. **Voice**: Deep, soft 'hoo huuuu', the first note sharp, second softer. (Namakwaduifie)

28 cm | **Br:** Jan–Dec   J F M A M J J A S O N D

Cape Parrot   E
This and the Grey-headed Parrot are the largest parrots in the region and confusion is unlikely because their ranges are mutually exclusive. Easily differentiated from Grey-headed Parrot by having a brown head. Female has a red forehead and both sexes have red shoulders and 'trousers'. **Habitat**: Forest and plantations; also commutes to orchards to feed. **Status**: Uncommon; usually in pairs or small flocks, often moving large distances to feed. **Voice**: Various loud, harsh screeches and squawks. (Woudpapegaai)

35 cm | **Br:** Sep–May   J F M A M J J A S O N D

Grey-headed Parrot
Replaces Cape Parrot in the N areas of the region. Differs from Cape Parrot by having an obvious grey, not brown head. Occurs sometimes in large, noisy flocks, especially on fruiting fig trees. **Habitat**: Broad-leaved woodland with large, emergent trees and riverine forests. **Status**: Locally common; usually in pairs or small groups, but large flocks gather at fruiting trees. **Voice**: Harsh shrieks and whistles, similar to Cape Parrot's. (Savannepapegaai)

36–38 cm | **Br:** Mar–Jun, Oct–Nov   J F M A M J J A S O N D

Brown-headed Parrot

A small, brown-headed parrot that at rest appears very green and is difficult to see in a leafy canopy; often it is the bird's screeches and squawks that indicate its presence. In flight, which is very rapid, the bright yellow underwings are visible. Imm. is a duller version of ad. **Habitat**: Savanna, riverine forests and open woodland. **Status**: Locally common. **Voice**: Typically parrot-like, raucous shriek. (Bruinkoppapegaai)

24–25 cm | Br: Mar–May   J F M A M J J A S O N D

Meyer's Parrot

The yellow bar across the crown on this small parrot, if present, is diagnostic. Differs from Brown-headed Parrot by having obvious yellow shoulder patches and bluish-green underparts. In flight shows much reduced yellow on underwing compared to Brown-headed Parrot. **Habitat**: Broad-leaved woodland and savanna. Flocks regularly congregate at waterholes. **Status**: Scarce to locally common. **Voice**: Loud, piercing 'chee-chee-chee-chee'; various other screeches and squawks. (Bosveldpapegaai)

21–33 cm | Br: Mar–Jun   J F M A M J J A S O N D

Rosy-faced Lovebird   NE

This Namibia special is a tiny parrot frequenting arid regions. Easily identified by its green colour, rosy-coloured face and blue rump. Difficult to locate in green leafy trees where they sit motionless. Usually detected by their screeching calls. **Habitat**: Dry, broad-leaved woodland, semi-desert and mountainous terrain; often breeds in Sociable Weaver nests. **Status**: Common. **Voice**: Typical parrot-like screeches and shrieks. (Rooiwangparkiet)

18 cm | Br: Feb–Apr, Oct   J F M A M J J A S O N D

Knysna Turaco   E

A large green bird with a long tail and crest. Distinguished from the Purple-crested Turaco by its greenish plumage, white-tipped crest and whitish marks above and below the eye. Groups frequent tree canopies where they run along the larger branches, raising and lowering their tails. In flight they show brilliant red patches on the wing tips. **Habitat**: Afromontane forest, from sea level in W, but at higher elevations in E. **Status**: Common. **Voice**: The call is a loud, far-carrying 'kow kow kow'. (Knysnaloerie)

40–42 cm | Br: Nov–Jan, Jun–Jul   J F M A M J J A S O N D

Purple-crested Turaco

Superficially resembles Knysna Turaco but is much darker. It has a dark purple crest that appears black unless seen in good light; lacks the white markings and crest tips of the Knysna Turaco and has bare red skin around eyes. It behaves very much like the Knysna Turaco in that it keeps to tree tops where it leaps from branch to branch, showing the bright red wing patches. **Habitat**: Coastal and riverine forests and broad-leaved woodland. **Status**: Common. **Voice**: Loud series of hollow 'kok-kok-kok-kok', typically longer and faster than other green turacos. (Bloukuifloerie)

43 cm | Br: Aug–Feb | J F M A M J J A S O N D

Grey Go-Away-Bird

A large, uniformly grey bird with a long tail and crest, it is often seen in groups perched on the top of thorn trees, where it looks like a giant mousebird. Flight is strong, with flapping alternating with gliding. Members of a group fly in single file, in follow-my-leader fashion. **Habitat**: Acacia savanna and dry, open woodland; also gardens. **Status**: Common; vocal and conspicuous; often seen in small groups perched on top of acacia trees. **Voice**: Harsh, nasal 'waaaay' or 'kay-waaaay' (rendered 'go-away'). (Kwêvoël)

48 cm | Br: Jan–Dec | J F M A M J J A S O N D

Narina Trogon

Although it is very brightly coloured, the bird habitually sits with its green back to the observer and is thus well camouflaged in its leafy surroundings. A front view will reveal the bright red breast and belly with a whitish undertail. Female lacks the green throat of male, has a duller crimson breast and is generally dowdier. **Habitat**: Forest, dense woodland and thickets. **Status**: Fairly common resident, with some local movements. **Voice**: Deep, hoarse 'hoo hook', with emphasis on second syllable, repeated 6–10 times; wags tail down slightly when calling. (Bosloerie)

30–34 cm | Br: Oct–Feb | J F M A M J J A S O N D

Common Cuckoo

Very difficult to tell apart from African Cuckoo. Main difference is in bill colour and in this species it is mostly dark with only a little yellow at the base. African Cuckoo shows a large expanse of yellow at the bill's base but this is very variable. **Habitat**: Woodland, savanna, riverine forests and plantations. **Status**: Scarce to locally common Palaearctic migrant Oct–Apr. **Voice**: Generally silent in Africa. (Europese koekoek)

32–34 cm | Br: n/a | J F M A M J J A S O N D

African Cuckoo

If seen well enough the undertail pattern on this species is barred while Common Cuckoo has a spotted pattern. It also shows a more extensive yellow base to the bill although this is a variable character. Easiest way to identify this species is by its 'oop oop' call. Common Cuckoo doesn't call in Africa. **Habitat**: Woodland and savanna. **Status**: Locally common intra-African migrant. **Voice**: Similar to African Hoopoe's 'hoop-hoop' call, but slower; female utters fast 'kik-kik-kik'. (Afrikaanse koekoek)

32–34 cm | Br: Sep–Dec | J F M A M J J A S O N D

Red-chested Cuckoo

This cuckoo's three-note call 'weet-weet-weeeoo' is diagnostic and is often the only indication of the bird's presence. It is normally only seen as it swiftly departs, when the very dark back and chestnut breast instantly identify it. Imm. is very dark above and is heavily barred black below. **Habitat**: Forests, plantations, woodland and gardens. **Status**: Common resident and intra-African migrant. **Voice**: Male calls monotonous 'weet-weet-weeoo' (rendered 'piet my vrou' in Afrikaans); female gives shrill 'pipipipipi'. (Piet-my-vrou)

28–31 cm | Br: Oct–Jan | J F M A M J J A S O N D

Black Cuckoo

More often heard than seen. It might be confused with its host, the Fork-tailed Drongo, but lacks the forked tail. It differs from the black morph Jacobin Cuckoo by lacking the crest and white wing patches. **Habitat**: Woodland, forest, plantations and gardens. **Status**: Common resident and intra-African migrant. **Voice**: Male song is mournful 'hoo hooee' or 'hoo hoo hooeee' (rendered 'I'm so sick'), with last note rising in pitch, repeated monotonously and sometimes ending in excited, rattling 'whurri whurri whurri'; female gives fast 'yow-yow-yow-yow'. (Swartkoekoek)

28–31 cm | Br: Oct–Nov | J F M A M J J A S O N D

Jacobin Cuckoo

An all-black morph occurs which might be mistaken for a Black Cuckoo but this species shows a diagnostic wispy crest and white patches at the base of the primaries. Pale phase birds are black and white with a long tail, crested head, white wing patches and lack any striping on the underparts. **Habitat**: Woodland, thickets and acacia savanna. **Status**: Common intra-African migrant, with some non-br. migrants from India. **Voice**: Shrill, repeated 'klee-klee-kleeuu-kleeuu', very similar to start of call of Levaillant's Cuckoo. (Bontnuwejaarsvoël)

33–34 cm | Br: Oct–Mar | J F M A M J J A S O N D

Great Spotted Cuckoo

A large and unmistakable cuckoo with a long, wedge-shaped tail, white-spotted back and grey crest. Juv. has a black, not grey crest, rich creamy throat and breast and in flight shows rufous primaries. Parasitises various species of starlings. Often seen being harrassed by its starling hosts, especially Red-winged Starling. **Habitat**: Woodland and savanna. **Status**: Fairly common intra-African migrant. **Voice**: Loud, far-carrying 'keeow-keeow-keeow'; shorter, crow-like 'kark'. (Gevlekte koekoek)

36–41 cm | **Br: Aug–Mar** | J F M A M J J A S O N D

Diderick Cuckoo

During summer the call is a familiar sound in and around the weaver and bishop colonies that these birds parasitise. They can be distinguished from Klaas's Cuckoo by their more contrasting bottle-green and white plumage, more extensive white behind the eye, and white flashes on the wings and shoulders. At close range the bright cherry-coloured eye can be seen. **Habitat**: Woodland, savanna, grassland and suburban gardens; near reed beds and weaver colonies. **Status**: Common resident and intra-African migrant. **Voice**: 'Dee-dee-deederic'. (Diederikkie)

17–19 cm | **Br: Oct–Apr** | J F M A M J J A S O N D

Klaas's Cuckoo

Confusable only with Diderick Cuckoo, from which it differs by having only a small white patch behind the eye, lacking white spotting on the wing coverts and having a brown, not red eye. Female differs from female Diderick Cuckoo by lacking wing spots and has a pale, not brownish throat. **Habitat**: Forests, woodland, savanna and gardens. **Status**: Common resident and intra-African migrant. **Voice**: Far-carrying 'huee-jee' (rendered in Afrikaans as 'meitjie'), repeated 3–6 times. (Meitjie)

16–18 cm | **Br: Sep–Apr** | J F M A M J J A S O N D

Burchell's Coucal   NE

Most often seen sitting on an exposed perch either drying itself after a downpour or sunning itself in the early morning. It is a large bird and is easily identified by its black cap, chestnut back and wings and long, black floppy tail. Some birds have a white-flecked head with a broad white eyebrow stripe. **Habitat**: Rank grass, riverine scrub, reed beds, thickets and gardens. **Status**: Common. **Voice**: The call, usually given before or after rain, is a liquid, bubbling series of notes. (Gewone vleiloerie)

40–41 cm | **Br: Sep–Mar** | J F M A M J J A S O N D

White-browed Coucal

Very similar to juv. Burchell's Coucal but fortunately their ranges do not overlap and confusion is hardly likely. The broad, creamy white eyebrow stripe and white-flecked crown, nape and mantle all help in identifying this species. **Habitat**: Reed beds and thickets, usually close to water. **Status**: Common. **Voice**: Liquid, bubbling 'doo-doo doo-doo', falling in pitch, then slowing and rising in pitch at end. (Gestreepte vleiloerie)

40–41 cm | Br: Sep–Mar   J F M A M J J A S O N D

Senegal Coucal

Very similar to Burchell's Coucal but is smaller and has a plain, not barred rump and base to tail. Juv. is probably not separable from juv. of either Burchell's or White-browed coucals. Creeps through undergrowth and thick tangles, but at onset of rains will perch exposed when calling. **Habitat**: Tangled vegetation and long grass; less tied to water than most other coucals. **Status**: Uncommon. **Voice**: Bubbling call note, very similar to that of Burchell's Coucal. (Senegalvleiloerie)

38–40 cm | Br: Oct–Mar   J F M A M J J A S O N D

Red-faced Mousebird

Easily distinguished from other mousebirds by being pale greyish in colour and by having the bill base and the naked skin around the eye bright red. Flight action is very different from that of other mousebirds in that it is direct, fast and powerful, with the birds flying in small groups or in single file. **Habitat**: Thornveld, open broad-leaved woodland and suburban gardens; avoids dense forest and desert. **Status**: Common resident. **Voice**: Clear, whistled 'chi vu vu', first note higher pitched. (Rooiwangmuisvoël)

34 cm | Br: Jan–Dec   J F M A M J J A S O N D

Speckled Mousebird

A small, drab, long-tailed bird that occurs in small groups and creeps about in bushes, mouse-like, and hangs from branches. When flushed, the birds fly to the next bush in follow-my-leader fashion and virtually crash-land. Distinguishable from the White-backed and Red-faced mousebirds by its black face, black-and-white bill, and brown legs. **Habitat**: Thick, tangled bush, and fruiting trees in gardens. **Status**: Common; usually in groups, often sunning after feeding or dashing between bushes. **Voice**: Harsh 'zhrrik-zhrrik'. (Gevlekte muisvoël)

35 cm | Br: Jan–Dec   J F M A M J J A S O N D

White-backed Mousebird E

Most likely to be confused with the Speckled Mousebird from which it is best differentiated at rest by having red legs and feet and a pale bill tipped with black. In flight the back shows a white stripe narrowly bordered with black and this is diagnostic. It behaves in much the same manner as the Speckled Mousebird but is more agile and has a more powerful flight. **Habitat**: Strandveld, fynbos and scrubby areas in semi-desert. **Status**: Common; usually in flocks of 3–10. **Voice**: Rather harsh, whistled 'zwee-wewit'. (Witkruismuisvoël)

34 cm | Br: Jan–Dec   J F M A M J J A S O N D

Alpine Swift

A very large, fast-flying swift and the only one in the region to have white underparts with a dark breast band. Sometimes gathers in large foraging flocks with other swift species when its large size is apparent alongside the much smaller African Black Swift. **Habitat**: Aerial and wide ranging. Breeds on high inland cliffs with vertical cracks. **Status**: Common resident and intra-African migrant, often in large flocks. **Voice**: Shrill scream. (Witpenswindswael)

21–22 cm | Br: Mar, Aug–Jan   J F M A M J J A S O N D

Common Swift

Very similar to African Black Swift, from which it differs only in having uniform dark upperwings and lacking the paler inner secondaries of that species. Often seen in large foraging flocks comprised of only this species, which is another pointer to their identification. **Habitat**: Aerial and wide ranging; often in large flocks; roosts on the wing. **Status**: Common Palaearctic migrant, mostly Oct–Mar. **Voice**: Shrill scream. (Europese windswael)

16–18 cm | Br: n/a   J F M A M J J A S O N D

African Black Swift

In good light and viewing conditions it is best told from the Common Swift by showing a pale patch at the base of the wings on the inner secondaries. When viewed from below this pale patch can be seen to be slightly translucent. **Habitat**: Aerial. Breeds in crevices on inland cliffs. During cold snaps in winter, will descend from higher ground to the coast, where they sometimes occur in very large flocks. **Status**: Common resident and intra-African migrant. **Voice**: High-pitched screaming. (Swartwindswael)

16–18 cm | Br: Sep–Feb   J F M A M J J A S O N D

Little Swift

A small, dumpy swift with a square-ended tail and broad white rump that wraps around the vent. Differs from White-rumped Swift by having a square-ended, not forked tail and a square, not U-shaped white rump. Occurs in large numbers when breeding. **Habitat:** Aerial; the most common swift over towns, often seen wheeling in tight flocks during display flights. Usually nests in colonies, under eaves of buildings and rocky overhangs. **Status:** Common resident, but subject to some movements in S. **Voice:** Soft twittering; high-pitched screeching. (Kleinwindswael)

12–14 cm | Br: Aug–Mar   J F M A M J J A S O N D

White-rumped Swift

The long, deeply forked tail combined with a narrow, U-shaped white rump is diagnostic. The forked tail is often held closed, which imparts a long, pointed tail effect. Does not usually occur in large flocks like Little Swift; normally found in pairs or small parties. **Habitat:** Aerial, over open country, often near water. Usually occupies Greater Striped Swallows' nests, and sometimes holes in buildings. **Status:** Common resident and intra-African migrant. **Voice:** Deeper screams than Little Swift's, and generally less vocal. (Witkruiswindswael)

14–15 cm | Br: Aug–Apr   J F M A M J J A S O N D

African Palm Swift

An exceptionally streamlined, thin swift with very long, deeply forked tail and very narrow scythe-like wings. Overall colour is greyish-brown. Tail usually held closed and appears pointed, but when stalling or on fast turns the tail is spread and shows the unusually deep fork. Most often seen around groups of palm trees in which it nests. **Habitat:** Aerial, usually in vicinity of palm trees, including those in towns. **Status:** Common resident and local migrant. **Voice:** Soft, high-pitched scream. (Palmwindswael)

17 cm | Br: Jan–Dec   J F M A M J J A S O N D

Red-breasted Swallow

This obviously very large swallow is readily identified by its conspicuous rufous underparts (diagnostic). In flight it can be seen that the red on the breast extends to the wing linings and forms a collar over the nape. The remainder of the plumage is a dark glossy blue and may appear black in some lights. Usually encountered in pairs along roadsides or in mixed flocks of swallows. **Habitat:** Found over open grassland in thornveld, and broad-leaved woodland and upland grassland. **Status:** Common summer visitor. **Voice:** Soft, warbling song; twittering notes in flight. (Rooiborsswael)

19–24 cm | Br: Aug–Apr   J F M A M J J A S O N D

South African Cliff Swallow   BrE

Confusable with juv. Lesser and Greater striped swallows but has only a slight notch on its square-ended tail and not the obvious forked tail of these two species. It further differs in having mottled, not streaked underparts and is more robust and chunky, with broader wings. The cap is dark, not chestnut. **Habitat**: Upland grassland, usually breeding in road bridges. **Status**: Locally common intra-African migrant. **Voice**: Twittering 'chooerp-chooerp'. (Familieswael)

15 cm | Br: Aug–Apr   J F M A M J J A S O N D

Greater Striped Swallow   BrE

Likely to be confused only with the Lesser Striped Swallow from which it is distinguished by being much larger, and by being far paler in overall appearance, with faint striping on white underparts discernible only at close range. The crown is pale orange and the pale rufous on the rump does not extend onto the vent. **Habitat**: Grassland and vleis. **Status**: Common intra-African migrant. Often seen near culverts, which it uses for breeding sites. **Voice**: Twittering 'chissick' and querulous, nasal notes. (Grootstreepswael)

20 cm | Br: Aug–Mar   J F M A M J J A S O N D

Lesser Striped Swallow

Noticeably smaller than the Greater Striped Swallow, it differs in plumage by being very heavily streaked on the underparts and by having a rich rufous rump that extends onto the vent. It also has a much richer rufous cap and nape. It occurs at lower altitudes than the Greater Striped Swallow and is frequently found in the vicinity of buildings, on which it builds its nest. **Habitat**: Usually near water. **Status**: Common resident and intra-African migrant. **Voice**: Descending series of squeaky, nasal 'zeh-zeh-zeh-zeh' notes. (Kleinstreepswael)

15–17 cm | Br: Oct–Jul   J F M A M J J A S O N D

Barn Swallow

Probably the commonest swallow in the region Nov–Mar; before migrating in March large numbers are often seen resting on telephone wires. They roost in dense reed beds, sometimes in hundreds of thousands. The ad. has a brick-red face and throat, a blue-black breast band and off-white to buffish underparts. The tail streamers are very long and there are white spots on the tail base. **Habitat**: Cosmopolitan, except in closed forest. **Status**: Abundant Palaearctic migrant, mostly Oct–Apr. **Voice**: Soft, high-pitched twittering. (Europese swael)

15–18 cm | Br: n/a   J F M A M J J A S O N D

Wire-tailed Swallow

Differs from White-throated Swallow by being smaller, slimmer and lacking a blue-black breast and has a bright chestnut cap, not just forehead. It also has a thin black band running across the vent. The very long and thin tail streamers are not easily seen in the field unless close to. **Habitat**: Usually near water, often breeding under bridges. **Status**: Common resident and intra-African migrant. **Voice**: Call is sharp, metallic 'tchik'; song is twittering 'chirrik-weet, chirrik-weet'. (Draadstertswael)

13–17 cm | Br: Jan–Dec J F M A M J J A S O N D

White-throated Swallow   **BrE**

The gleaming white throat contrasts with the black breast band and greyish underparts. A small red patch on the forehead is visible at close range. The remainder of the plumage is a glossy blue-black, and white spots are visible in the centre of the tail when the bird banks in flight. **Habitat**: Closely associated with water. It is usually seen in pairs, generally near water, nesting under bridges and road culverts. **Status**: Common intra-African migrant. **Voice**: Soft warbles and twitters. (Witkeelswael)

14–17 cm | Br: Aug–Apr J F M A M J J A S O N D

Pearl-breasted Swallow

Easily distinguished from Wire-tailed Swallow by having a dark blue, not bright chestnut cap and lacking long, thin tail streamers and a black band across the vent. Might be momentarily mistaken for Common House-Martin but has a dark, not white rump and has white, not dark underwing linings. Juv. is less glossy blue than ad. **Habitat**: Grassland, savanna and open woodland; often breeds in buildings. **Status**: Locally common resident and migrant in the S. **Voice**: Subdued chipping note in flight. (Pêrelborsswael)

14 cm | Br: Aug–Mar J F M A M J J A S O N D

Black Saw-wing

An all-sooty black swallow with a deeply forked tail. The plumage is mostly matt black but shows some slight gloss on the mantle. The smaller size and slow, fluttering flight should rule out confusion with any dark swifts in the region. Female has a shorter forked tail than male and juv. is very dark brown with a shorter forked tail. **Habitat**: Fringes and clearings in forests and plantations. **Status**: Locally common. **Voice**: Soft 'chrrp' alarm call. (Swartsaagvlerkswael)

13–15 cm | Br: Sep–Mar J F M A M J J A S O N D

Common House Martin

The only swallow-like bird in the region to have totally white underparts and white rump. Differs from similar Pearl-breasted Swallow by having a white, not dark rump. Juv. is similar to ad. but the rump is greyish, not white. At close range the legs and toes can be seen to be feathered, a unique feature to this martin. **Habitat**: Over most open habitats; often feeds higher in the sky than most other swallows. **Status**: Common Palaearctic migrant Sep–Apr; has been known to breed in South Africa. **Voice**: Single 'chirrp'. (Huisswael)

14 cm | Br: n/a   J F M A M J J A S O N D

Banded Martin

Confusion with Sand Martin most likely but is noticeably much larger, has very obvious white, not dark wing linings, has a small white eyebrow stripe and a square-ended, not forked tail. It invariably shows a thin brown line running across the base of the undertail. Juv. has the upperparts scaled with buff. **Habitat**: Areas of low vegetation or grassland. **Status**: Locally common resident and intra-African migrant. **Voice**: Flight call is 'che-che-che'; song is jumble of harsh 'chip-choops'. (Gebande oewerswael)

15–17 cm | Br: Aug–May   J F M A M J J A S O N D

Sand Martin

Confusion most likely with Brown-throated Martin but differs by having a distinctive white throat and brown breast band. Differs from similarly marked Banded Martin but is smaller and has all-dark, not white, wing linings, a forked, not square-ended tail and lacks a white eyebrow stripe. **Habitat**: Usually over or near fresh water. **Status**: Locally common Palaearctic migrant Oct–Mar; scarce in extreme SW. **Voice**: Grating 'chrrr'. (Europese oewerswael)

11–12 cm | Br: n/a   J F M A M J J A S O N D

Brown-throated Martin

Occurs in two colour forms. An all-dark brown bird with small amounts of white on the undertail and paler version with large amounts of white from lower breast to undertail. Confusable with Sand Martin but lacks a white throat and has uniform brown throat and upper breast. **Habitat**: Open areas, usually near water; breeds in sandbanks. **Status**: Common. **Voice**: Soft twittering. (Afrikaanse oewerswael)

11–12 cm | Br: Jan–Dec   J F M A M J J A S O N D

Rock Martin

A medium-sized martin and the only one with all-brown plumage. It could be confused with the dark form of the Brown-throated Martin, but that species is smaller and shows a white belly and vent. The Rock Martin has the underparts slightly paler than the upperparts and, in flight, white spots are visible on the spread tail. **Habitat**: It prefers rocky and mountainous terrain but has adapted to towns and cities, where it nests freely on buildings. **Status**: Common. **Voice**: Soft, high-pitched twitterings. (Kransswael)

12–15 cm | Br: Jan–Dec   J F M A M J J A S O N D

Giant Kingfisher

This huge kingfisher is unmistakable with its massive bill, dark upperparts finely spotted with white and bright chestnut breast band. Female has all-chestnut underparts and both sexes show chestnut wing linings in flight. Imm. has dark, streaked breast and chestnut flanks. **Habitat**: Wooded streams and dams, fast-flowing rivers and coastal lagoons. **Status**: Common. **Voice**: Loud, harsh 'kahk-kah-kahk'. (Reusevisvanger)

juv.

38–43 cm | Br: Aug–Jan   J F M A M J J A S O N D

Pied Kingfisher

The only kingfisher to have a pied black and white plumage. The bill is exceptionally long. Male has a double black breast band whereas female has only a single. Before plunging for its fish prey, this species either perches on a branch overhanging water or it hovers and then dives. It sometimes occurs in small groups whose members interact excitedly, giving a twittering call. **Habitat**: Any open stretch of fresh water, coastal lagoons and tidal pools. **Status**: Common. **Voice**: Rattling twitter; sharp, high-pitched 'chik-chik'. (Bontvisvanger)

23–25 cm | Br: Jan–Dec   J F M A M J J A S O N D

♀

Malachite Kingfisher

Usually seen fleetingly as it passes low over the water. When fishing, remains motionless for long periods, perched on a reed stem or branch overhanging water, and is often overlooked. The crown is barred black and turquoise, the back is an iridescent blue with a turquoise rump, and the underparts are reddish-brown and white. The bill in the ad. is bright red and is a useful identification feature, but imm. has a blackish bill. **Habitat**: Lakes and dams, and along streams and lagoons. **Status**: Common resident. **Voice**: High-pitched 'peep-peep' in flight. (Kuifkopvisvanger)

13–14 cm | Br: Jan–Dec   J F M A M J J A S O N D

African Pygmy Kingfisher

This tiny kingfisher rarely frequents wetland habitats and is usually found away from water in forest and woodland areas. It differs from the Malachite Kingfisher by its smaller size, orangey eyebrow and violet wash across the cheeks and face. More often heard than seen. Sometimes sits for long periods, low down in a tree or bush. **Habitat**: Woodland, savanna and coastal forest. **Status**: Common resident and intra-African migrant. **Voice**: High-pitched 'chip-chip' flight note. (Dwergvisvanger)

12–13 cm | **Br: Sep–Mar**   J F M A M J J A S O N D

Woodland Kingfisher

Much more brightly coloured than the Brown-hooded Kingfisher and has a black lower mandible and red upper mandible, not an all-red bill. Differs further from the Brown-hooded Kingfisher by having a blue head, back and tail. Often seen perched on a tree top displaying with outstretched wings and giving its sharp, piercing 'trrp-trrrrrrrr' call. Imm. is dowdier and its black lower mandible shows some red patches. **Habitat**: Woodland and savanna. **Status**: Common resident and intra-African migrant. **Voice**: Loud, piercing 'chip-cherrrrrrrrr', descending. (Bosveldvisvanger)

20–22 cm | **Br: Oct–Mar**   J F M A M J J A S O N D

Brown-hooded Kingfisher

A much duller bird than other red-billed kingfishers. Easily identified by its all-red bill, brownish, streaked head, chestnut patches on the sides of the breast, and streaked flanks. Shows less blue on wings and lower back than the Woodland Kingfisher, but this is still very evident in flight. Sits motionless on perch waiting for prey and in a blue flash will descend rapidly to the ground to snatch an insect or lizard. **Habitat**: Woodland, coastal forests, parks and gardens. **Status**: Common. **Voice**: Whistled 'tyi-ti-ti-ti'; harsher 'klee-klee-klee' alarm note. (Bruinkopvisvanger)

19–20 cm | **Br: Sep–Apr**   J F M A M J J A S O N D

Striped Kingfisher

A small, dull bushveld kingfisher that is easily recognised by its dark-capped appearance which contrasts with a pale collar, the fine streaking on its breast, and a red-and-black bill. The call is a high-pitched 'cheer-cherrrrr' and, when calling in display, it will raise its wings to show the black-and-white patterned underwing and blue back. The latter is more obvious in flight. **Habitat**: Woodland, savanna and forest edge. **Status**: Common. **Voice**: High-pitched, piercing 'cheer-cherrrrrrrrr'. (Gestreepte visvanger)

16–18 cm | **Br: Sep–Feb**   J F M A M J J A S O N D

European Bee-eater

In flight this bird shows a dazzling array of colours with its chestnut to golden back contrasting with turquoise-blue underparts and almost translucent, rufous wings. At rest the bright yellow throat bordered by a narrow black gorget can be seen. Imm. has a greenish back and pale blue underparts. **Habitat**: Frequents thornveld, broad-leaved woodland and adjacent grassy areas. **Status**: Common migrant in summer. Breeds in Cape. **Voice**: Characteristic, far-carrying peawhistle-like 'prrrup' call. (Europese byvreter)

26–28 cm | Br: Aug–Jan **J F M A M J J A S O N D**

Blue-cheeked Bee-eater

This green-and-blue bee-eater is easily recognised by its green cap, blue facial markings and orange throat. In flight it shows orange underwings. In worn plumage the blue facial marking can appear white. Imm. is duller than ad. and lacks the pointed tail projections. **Habitat**: Flood plains and adjacent woodlands. **Status**: Fairly common migrant from Sep–Apr. **Voice**: Liquid 'prrup' and 'preoo'; less mellow than European Bee-eater. (Blouwangbyvreter)

23–31 cm | Br: n/a **J F M A M J J A S O N D**

White-fronted Bee-eater

In flight appears very green with a dark blue undertail, but at rest the red-and-white throat and white forehead are diagnostic. Has a square-ended tail and lacks pointed tail projections. Hunts insects from a perch, sallying forth to take prey in flight, and then returns to the same perch. **Habitat**: Nest colonies, which are sometimes large, are situated in steep sandy cliffs cut by wide, slow-moving rivers. **Status**: Common. **Voice**: The birds are active and noisy around the nests, giving nasal 'qrrruk-qrruk' calls. (Rooikeelbyvreter)

22–24 cm | Br: Apr–May, Aug–Dec **J F M A M J J A S O N D**

Southern Carmine Bee-eater

Unmistakable large, pinkish bee-eater with long tail projections. Has a turquoise crown and in flight shows a pale blue vent and rump. Juv. is overall duller with a brown back; lacks the tail projections and sometimes shows a bluish throat. **Habitat**: Woodland, savanna and flood plains. Breeds colonially in river banks. **Status**: Common resident and local migrant. **Voice**: Deep 'terk, terk'. (Rooiborsbyvreter)

imm.

26–36 cm | Br: Aug–Dec **J F M A M J J A S O N D**

Swallow-tailed Bee-eater

The only bee-eater in the region to have a forked tail. Might be confused with smaller Little Bee-eater but has a blue, not black collar, blue-green underparts and a forked blue tail and rump. Juv. has the diagnostic forked tail but is duller and lacks the blue collar and yellow throat. **Habitat**: Wide range, from semi-desert scrub to forest margins. **Status**: Common resident with local movements. **Voice**: 'Kwit-kwit'; soft twittering. (Swaelstertbyvreter)

19–22 cm | **Br: Aug–Feb** J F M A M J J A S O N D

Little Bee-eater

The smallest bee-eater and probably the most widespread and common. Easily identified by its small size, green back and buffy underparts, yellow throat with black gorget, and square or slightly forked tail that lacks projections. The russet underwings are conspicuous when the bird dashes out to catch insects. **Habitat**: Savanna, woodland, forest edge and around wetlands. **Status**: Common; usually in pairs or small groups. **Voice**: 'Zeet-zeet' or 'chip-chip'. (Kleinbyvreter)

14–17 cm | **Br: Aug–Feb** J F M A M J J A S O N D

Lilac-breasted Roller

This species is commonly seen in some game reserves. It frequently perches on telephone poles and wires, from where it swoops to catch its insect prey. In flight it shows a range of pale and dark blues in the wing. At rest, the lilac breast and long, pointed outer-tail feathers are diagnostic. When displaying, male will perform a complex flight in which he rolls from side to side on the downward stoop. **Habitat**: Savanna. Perches conspicuously. **Status**: Common resident and local migrant. **Voice**: Harsh squawks and screams. (Gewone troupant)

32–36 cm | **Br: Aug–Feb** J F M A M J J A S O N D

European Roller

Superficially resembles the Lilac-breasted Roller but lacks the long outer-tail feathers of that species and has a clear blue breast and much more chestnut on the back. In flight it appears paler than the Lilac-breasted Roller and has a square-ended tail. Although imm. Lilac-breasted Roller has a square-ended tail, it has a lilac-washed breast. Catches insects on the wing or by swooping from a perch to the ground. **Habitat**: Savanna. **Status**: Common Palaearctic migrant Oct–Mar. **Voice**: Normally silent in Africa; 'krack-krack' call when alarmed. (Europese troupant)

30–31 cm | **Br: n/a** J F M A M J J A S O N D

Purple Roller
A large, robust roller that has a pale forehead and eyebrow stripe and dark, lilac-brown underparts heavily striped with white. In flight shows deep wings and tail. Juv. similar to ad. but is overall duller and has darker underparts. **Habitat**: Dry thornveld and open, broad-leaved woodland. **Status**: Scarce to common resident and intra-African migrant. **Voice**: Harsh, repeated 'karaa-karaa' in display flight, accompanied by exaggerated, side-to-side rocking motion. (Groottroupant)

33–38 cm | Br: Aug–Apr   J F M A M J J A S O N D

Broad-billed Roller
The smallest and darkest roller and easily told by its bright yellow bill. In flight shows a short, pale blue tail with a dark central stripe and tip. The flight feathers are different shades of dark blue with dark purple underwings. Partly crepuscular; sometimes birds aerially hawk insects over the wooded canopy. **Habitat**: Riverine forests and adjacent savanna. Often perches and breeds in dead trees. **Status**: Locally common resident and intra-African migrant. **Voice**: Harsh screams and cackles. (Geelbektroupant)

27–28 cm | Br: Aug–Apr   J F M A M J J A S O N D

Southern Ground-Hornbill
Unmistakable. A large, black, turkey-sized bird with bright red, naked face and throat and a large, decurved black bill. Walks on highly arched toes. In flight shows conspicuous white ends to the wings. Imm. has buffy yellow, naked face and throat. **Habitat**: Savanna, woodland and grassland with adjoining forests. **Status**: Scarce; occurs in family groups. Now mainly confined to large reserves and national parks. **Voice**: Loud, booming 'ooomph ooomph' early in the morning. (Bromvoël)

90–100 cm | Br: Aug–Jan   J F M A M J J A S O N D

Trumpeter Hornbill
This large black-and-white hornbill is instantly recognisable by its black bill and large casque, and its red face. Female and imm. have smaller casques, pied plumage similar to that of male, and reddish faces. The species has a dipping flight action, with noisy wing flapping interspersed with glides. **Habitat**: Lowland, coastal and riverine evergreen forests. **Status**: Common resident and local nomad. **Voice**: Wailing, plaintive 'waaaaa-weeeee-waaaaa', resembling the sound of a baby crying. (Gewone boskraai)

58–60 cm | Br: Sep–Jan   J F M A M J J A S O N D

Monteiro's Hornbill   NE

This Namibia special is easily identified by the white-spotted forewings and in flight by the conspicuous white wing patches and broad white outer-tail feathers. The bill is variable in size, depending on sex and age, sometimes growing into a very long, heavily decurved shape. **Habitat**: Dry thornveld and broad-leaved woodland. **Status**: Common resident and local nomad. **Voice**: Hollow-sounding 'tooaak tooaak', uttered with head lowered and wings closed. (Monteironeushoringvoël)

56 cm | **Br: Oct–Apr**   J F M A M J J A S O N D

Crowned Hornbill

Very similar to Monteiro's Hornbill but is overall much darker. The bill is shorter with an obvious casque and the eye is pale yellow, not dark as in Monteiro's Hornbill. At close range a dull yellow base to the bill can be seen. Outside br. season, sometimes gathers in large flocks in fruiting trees. **Habitat**: Inland, coastal and riverine forests. **Status**: Common resident and local nomad in dry season; often in flocks. **Voice**: Whistling 'chleeoo chleeoo'. (Gekroonde neushoringvoël)

54 cm | **Br: Sep–Jan**   J F M A M J J A S O N D

African Grey Hornbill

The only small hornbill that has a dark bill. Female might be mistaken for a Southern Yellow-billed Hornbill because the top of her bill is creamy yellow, but she has a dark head and breast, and a conspicuous white eyebrow stripe. Imm. is very similar to female. Flight action is very floppy and buoyant. **Habitat**: Acacia savanna and dry, broad-leaved woodland. **Status**: Common. **Voice**: Plaintive, whistling 'phee pheeoo phee pheeoo', with bill held vertically and wings flicked open on each note. (Grysneushoringvoël)

46–51 cm | **Br: Sep–Mar**   J F M A M J J A S O N D

Southern Yellow-billed Hornbill

Resembles Southern Red-billed Hornbill but is far larger and has a more massive yellow, not red bill. The female African Grey Hornbill, which has a creamy yellow top to her bill and might be confused with this species, has a dark head and breast. Feeds mostly on the ground where it hops, not walks. **Habitat**: Thornveld and dry, broad-leaved woodland. **Status**: Common. **Voice**: Rapid, hollow-sounding 'tok tok tok tok tok tokatokatoka', uttered with head lowered and wings fanned. (Geelbekneushoringvoël)

55 cm | **Br: Sep–Mar**   J F M A M J J A S O N D

Southern Red-billed Hornbill

Plumage resembles the Southern Yellow-billed Hornbill's but this species has a shorter, more slender, red bill. Distinguished from all other hornbills with red bills by its small size. Imm. has a duller, less well-developed bill and has buff, not white spotting on the wings. **Habitat**: Savanna and semi-arid woodland. **Status**: Locally common. **Voice**: Display consists of the bird bobbing its head and giving a long series of 'kuk kuk kuk' calls, becoming faster and louder, ending with double notes 'kuk-we kuk-we'. (Rooibekneushoringvoël)

40–51 cm | Br: Sep–Mar J F M A M J J A S O N D

Green Wood-Hoopoe

The ad. is a large, glossy blue-and-green bird with a long, graduated, white-tipped tail and a long, red, decurved bill and red feet. Imm. is not as glossy as ad. and has a black, not red bill. Small groups clamber through foliage and up tree trunks, using their bills to probe for insects. **Habitat**: Wide variety of woodland, thicket and forest edge. **Status**: Common. **Voice**: The cackling call is sometimes given by the whole group; birds sway backwards and forwards while calling. (Rooibekkakelaar)

32–36 cm | Br: Jan–Dec J F M A M J J A S O N D

Common Scimitarbill

Likely to be confused only with imm. Green Wood-Hoopoe, which has a black bill, but this species is smaller and its bill is much thinner and more decurved. In flight the white patches in the wings and the long, graduated, white-tipped tail can be seen. It appears black at a distance but, in direct sunlight, the glossy purple-and-blue plumage is evident. **Habitat**: Dry savanna and open, broad-leaved woodland. **Status**: Common. **Voice**: High-pitched, whistling 'sweep-sweep-sweep'; harsher chattering. (Swartbekkakelaar)

28–30 cm | Br: Aug–Feb J F M A M J J A S O N D

African Hoopoe

The combination of a pinkish-brown body and striking black-and-white wings and tail is diagnostic. The black- and white-tipped crest is often held closed but the bird will raise it if alarmed or on alighting. When feeding it walks with a jerky gait and probes its long bill into the ground, searching for insects. **Habitat**: Savanna, broad-leaved woodland, parks and gardens. **Status**: Common. **Voice**: 'Hoop-hoop-hoop', typically all notes at same pitch. (Hoephoep)

25–28 cm | Br: Aug–Feb J F M A M J J A S O N D

Greater Honeyguide

Male has a black throat which, combined with a dark cap, imparts a white ear patch effect. Female is a duller version of male and lacks the head pattern, and juv. shows creamy underparts. **Habitat**: Woodland, savanna and plantations; avoids forests. **Status**: Scarce to locally common. **Voice**: Ringing, repeated 'whit-purr' or 'vic-tor' from regularly used site high in tree; guiding call is harsh, rattling chatter. (Grootheuningwyser)

18–20 cm | Br: Apr, Sep–Jan | J F M A M J J A S O N D

Lesser Honeyguide

It is overall dull greyish, with a greenish wash on the wing coverts, a small dark moustachial stripe and conspicuous white outer-tail feathers. It is often seen being harassed by barbets and, as it dashes through the canopy, its white tail feathers are conspicuous. **Habitat**: Well-wooded habitats from forest to dense savanna; has adapted to suburban gardens. **Status**: Common. **Voice**: Characteristic 'frip', repeated 15–40 times at short intervals; same call site is used regularly. (Kleinheuningwyser)

13–15 cm | Br: Sep–Feb | J F M A M J J A S O N D

Black-collared Barbet

Instantly recognisable by the bright red face and throat broadly bordered with black. This bulbul-sized bird has a short tail, chunky body and very thick bill. Imm. has the face and throat brown, streaked with red and orange. **Habitat**: Forests, woodland, savanna and gardens. **Status**: Common; often in groups. **Voice**: Pairs duet in display by sitting together and bobbing up and down; the call starts with a harsh 'krrr krrrr', followed by ringing 'tooo puudly tooo puudly', the 'tooo' being higher pitched. (Rooikophoutkapper)

18–20 cm | Br: Aug–Apr | J F M A M J J A S O N D

White-eared Barbet

An overall very dark barbet with diagnostic white ear patches and white belly. Juv. shows a slightly paler back and has a distinctly pale base to the robust bill. Very often seen in small groups. **Habitat**: Coastal forest and bush, often near rivers. **Status**: Common; usually in groups. **Voice**: Loud, twittering 'treee treeetee teeetree'; harsher 'waa waa' notes. (Witoorhoutkapper)

17–18 cm | Br: Aug–Apr | J F M A M J J A S O N D

Crested Barbet

The largest of the barbets, this species is unmistakable with its orange-yellow face, black shaggy crest and broad black breast band, white- and golden-speckled back, and crimson rump. Much more terrestrial than other barbets, it hops around with an upright stance, but when it does fly, the flight is rapid and direct. **Habitat**: Occurs in open, broad leaved woodland, thornveld and riverine forest; has adapted to suburban gardens. **Status**: Common. **Voice**: The song is a diagnostic trilling which has been likened to the ringing of a muffled alarm clock. (Kuifkophoutkapper)

23–24 cm | Br: Jan–Dec   J F M A M J J A S O N D

Acacia Pied Barbet

Similar in shape to the Black-collared Barbet but is smaller and has diagnostic black and-white plumage, a red forehead and yellow spotting on the back and wings. Might be confused with the Red-fronted Tinkerbird but is much larger, has a black bib and more massive bill. Mostly solitary or in pairs. **Habitat**: Woodland and savanna, especially arid acacia woodland; also gardens. **Status**: Common. **Voice**: Nasal 'nehh, nehh, nehh' (toy trumpet) call, repeated 3–5 times; soft, low-pitched 'poop-oop-oop-oop…'. (Bonthoutkapper)

16–18 cm | Br: Aug–Apr   J F M A M J J A S O N D

Yellow-fronted Tinkerbird

Very similar to Red-fronted Tinkerbird but their ranges hardly overlap so confusion isn't likely. The yellow forehead is diagnostic but is variable and can appear orangey-red, but never the bright red of Red-fronted Tinkerbird. It is also overall paler and lacks the yellow wing patches of Red-fronted Tinkerbird. **Habitat**: Woodland and savanna. **Status**: Common. **Voice**: Continuous 'pop-pop-pop …' or 'tink tink tink' very similar to Red-fronted Tinkerbird's. (Geelblestinker)

11 cm | Br: May, Jul–Mar   J F M A M J J A S O N D

Yellow-rumped Tinkerbird

The combination of black crown and back with bold white stripes on the face easily identify this tiny barbet. The bright yellow rump is not easily seen in the field. **Habitat**: Forest, forest edge and dense woodland. **Status**: Common. **Voice**: 'Pop pop pop pop'; a lower-pitched, more ringing note than that of Red- or Yellow-fronted tinkerbirds, repeated in phrases of 4–6 notes, not continuously. (Swartblestinker)

9–11 cm | Br: Jan–Dec   J F M A M J J A S O N D

Red-fronted Tinkerbird

Easily identified by its diagnostic bright red forehead. Overall much darker than Yellow-fronted Tinkerbird and shows a bold yellowish-gold forewing. The distribution of these two similar tiny barbets hardly overlap so confusion is not likely. **Habitat**: Coastal forests in S, more arid woodland and thickets in N. **Status**: Common. **Voice**: Continuous, monotonous 'pop-pop-pop…', very similar to Yellow-fronted Tinkerbird's, but slightly faster and higher pitched. (Rooiblestinker)

9–10.5 cm | **Br**: Aug–Jan   J F M A M J J A S O N D

Red-throated Wryneck

A woodpecker-like bird with richly patterned upperparts and a diagnostic rufous throat patch. Juv. has a much paler rufous throat patch. Moves jerkily along branches and feeds chiefly on the ground. **Habitat**: Grassland and open savanna, woodland and forest edge; has adapted well to suburban gardens and plantations (especially eucalyptus). **Status**: Locally common within its disjunct range. **Voice**: Series of 2–10 squeaky 'kweek' notes; also repeated, scolding 'peegh'. (Draaihals)

19 cm | **Br**: Apr–Feb   J F M A M J J A S O N D

Ground Woodpecker   E

The only woodpecker in the region that is almost entirely terrestrial. It will occasionally clamber into shrubs and small trees. It is easily identified by its diagnostic pinkish-red breast and rump. Male is much more brightly coloured than female, with a larger expanse of pink on belly and rump. **Habitat**: Rocky hill slopes in fynbos, Karoo and grassland; not associated with trees. **Status**: Common; usually in small family parties. **Voice**: Far-carrying 'aargh' or 'pee-aargh'; ringing 'ree-chick'. (Grondspeg)

25 cm | **Br**: Jul–Dec   J F M A M J J A S O N D

Olive Woodpecker

The combination of grey head and a dull green body is diagnostic on this easily identified woodpecker. Male shows a red crown and nape and juv. male has freckled red crown and nape. **Habitat**: Forests and dense woodland, often in small forest patches and near forest edge. **Status**: Common. **Voice**: Loud, cheerful 'wir-rit', repeated at intervals. (Gryskopspeg)

16–18 cm | **Br**: Aug–Nov   J F M A M J J A S O N D

Cardinal Woodpecker

Very much smaller than the Golden-tailed Woodpecker and the smallest woodpecker in the region. Sometimes difficult to locate when feeding in thick bush or leafy canopy but its incessant tapping on a branch often reveals its position. Paler and less streaked below than the Golden-tailed Woodpecker, it has a buff and yellow-barred, not spotted back. Flight action is fast and undulating. **Habitat**: Arid and semi-arid woodland, savanna and gardens. **Status**: Locally common. **Voice**: Weak, high-pitched trill. (Kardinaalspeg)

14–15 cm | Br: Jul–Dec   J F M A M J J A S O N D   ♀

Golden-tailed Woodpecker

The loud, nasal 'wheeeeeeaa' shriek and bill tapping on wood often reveal the presence of this bird. When it is seen clinging to a tree, the best identification features to look for are the streaked underparts, buff and yellow spots on the olive back, and the black-and-red crown and red moustachial stripe. It climbs vertical tree trunks with jerky movements, using its tail as a brace. **Habitat**: Woodland, thickets and coastal forests. **Status**: Common. **Voice**: Loud, nasal shriek, 'wheeeeeaa'. (Goudstertspeg)

18–20 cm | Br: Aug–Dec   J F M A M J J A S O N D   ♀

Bennett's Woodpecker

Male has diagnostic reddish-flecked forehead and moustachial stripes. Female has rusty-coloured throat and ear patches and heavily spotted underparts. The flight is direct with deep undulations; wings flapped and then held close to the body. Forages mostly on the ground. **Habitat**: Broad-leaved woodland and savanna. **Status**: Scarce to common. **Voice**: High-pitched, chattering 'whirrr-itt, whrrr-itt', often uttered in duet. (Bennettspeg)

18–20 cm | Br: Aug–Feb   J F M A M J J A S O N D   ♀

Bearded Woodpecker

A large, robust woodpecker with a boldly patterned black-and-white face. Male has a red crown and both sexes have very dark underparts, finely barred grey and white. During the br. season, the male will often sit on an exposed dead branch, drumming for long periods. **Habitat**: Woodland, riverine forests and thickets, favouring areas with dead trees; avoids dense forest. **Status**: Common. **Voice**: Loud, rapid 'wik-wik-wik-wik'; drums very loudly. (Baardspeg)

23–25 cm | Br: Apr–Dec   J F M A M J J A S O N D   ♀

Flappet Lark
This bird's aerial display flight is diagnostic. It flies high, rattling its wings in a series of short bursts. Display flight can last for several minutes before the bird plummets to earth. Eastern form is much darker than western form and both have heavily mottled backs and rufous patches in the wings. **Habitat**: Grassland, savanna and woodland with at least some openings. **Status**: Common; occurs in pairs. **Voice**: Short 'tuee'. Display flight includes brief bursts of rapid wing-clapping (2–3 phrases, separated by several seconds), but no song. (Laeveldklappertjie)

14–15 cm | **Br:** Oct–Apr   J F M A M J J A S O N D

Sabota Lark
A small, nondescript lark that has no obvious display flight or diagnostic song. Its habit of sitting on small trees and telephone wires and delivering its jumbled song full of mimicry are pointers to its identification. It has a short, thick bill, a buff or white eyebrow stripe that imparts a capped appearance, and it lacks the rufous wing patches seen in many other similar species. **Habitat**: Arid savanna and Nama Karoo. **Status**: Common. **Voice**: Jumbled song of rich, melodious 'chips' and twitterings; mimics other birds; often calls from elevated perch. (Sabotalewerik)

15 cm | **Br:** Oct–May   J F M A M J J A S O N D

Fawn-coloured Lark
Colour is variable from region to region but white underparts with a string of faint streaks across the breast is diagnostic. When singing, it perches on a branch, telephone wire or post and sits crouched in an almost horizontal position, pointing its head and bill slightly up and from side to side. **Habitat**: Sandy soils in Kalahari scrub, broad-leaved woodland and thornveld. **Status**: Fairly common. **Voice**: Jumble of harsh 'chips' and twitterings, ending in buzzy slur, given from tree top or during short display flight; occasionally mimics other birds' songs. (Vaalbruinlewerik)

14–16 cm | **Br:** Sep–Apr   J F M A M J J A S O N D

Large-billed Lark   E
The large, thick and robust bill with a yellow base to the lower mandible is diagnostic. This is a large, chunky and robust lark with a short, dark tail and very heavily streaked underparts. Its short crest is only visible when the bird is alarmed or singing. Sings from mounds of earth or sometimes fence posts or wire. **Habitat**: Grass and scrublands, and open and fallow fields. **Status**: Common. **Voice**: Highly vocal; far-carrying, ascending 'troo-lee-lii', like a rusty gate being opened; mimics other species. (Dikbeklewerik)

18 cm | **Br:** Feb, Apr, Aug–Dec   J F M A M J J A S O N D

Rufous-naped Lark

Most often seen during br. season when it perches on small bushes or termite mounds singing a simple 'treelee-treelooe' phrase. Often flicks its wings during song phrase. It less regularly gives a display flight during which the song becomes a jumbled chattering. Best recognised by its calls, combined with a rufous nape and large rufous wing patches, which are conspicuous when the bird flushes. **Habitat**: Grassland and savanna; also cultivated fields. **Status**: Common and widespread. **Voice**: Perched, gives frequently repeated, three-syllabled 'tree tree-leeooo'. (Rooineklewerik)

15–18 cm | **Br**: Jul–Apr   J F M A M J J A S O N D

Red-capped Lark

A conspicuous and sometimes very common lark that gathers in flocks outside the br. season. Colour can vary from area to area but the combination of a red cap and red shoulder smudges is diagnostic. The underparts are white to off-white and clear, unlike those of any other lark in the region. **Habitat**: Found in a wide range of habitats from desert to moist grasslands. **Status**: Common. **Voice**: The call given by flocks in flight is a sparrow like 'tchweerp'; song is a jumbled mixture of melodious notes. (Rooikoplewerik)

14–15 cm | **Br**: Jul–Apr   J F M A M J J A S O N D

Cape Long-billed Lark   E

This bird has the longest bill of the long billed larks. It is also the most patterned, with heavily streaked upperparts and underparts. The streaking on the underparts extends well onto belly and flanks. Female is smaller than male and has a noticeably shorter bill. Display flight common to all long-billed larks; bird flies close to ground then swings up vertically for 10–15 m, closes its wings, calls and then drops. **Habitat**: Coastal dunes and croplands. **Status**: Fairly common. **Voice**: Song is a far-carrying, descending whistle 'seeeeoooo'. (Weskuslangbeklewerik)

20–24 cm | **Br**: Aug–Oct   J F M A M J J A S O N D

Eastern Long-billed Lark   E

The smallest of the long-billed larks and the plainest in colour. Upperparts are reddish, slightly streaked in the W and uniform in the E. Underparts virtually unstreaked with a slight suffuse on the breast. Has the shortest, slimmest and straightest bill, which imparts a pipit-like appearance. **Habitat**: Grassland, generally on rocky hill slopes. **Status**: Fairly common. **Voice**: Long, descending whistle 'seeeeoooo'. (Grasveldlangbeklewerik)

16–20 cm | **Br**: Sep–Jan   J F M A M J J A S O N D

Chestnut-backed Sparrow-Lark

Similar to Grey-backed Sparrowlark but differs by having a rich chestnut, not grey back and wholly black crown. Female is mottled with buff and brown above and has a dark belly patch. Best told from female Grey-backed Sparrowlark by having chestnut, not greyish-brown wing coverts. **Habitat**: Sparsely grassed savanna and cultivated lands, especially near burned areas. **Status**: Common but nomadic and usually in flocks. **Voice**: Short 'chiop-chew' flight call. (Rooiruglewerik)

12–13 cm | **Br**: Jan–Dec | J F M A M J J A S O N D

Grey-backed Sparrow-Lark   NE

When seen on the ground the diagnostic coloration of totally black underparts, greyish upperparts and black-and-white patterned head are clearly visible. Female is small and squat like male, also has a pale conical bill and greyish upperparts, but has only a patch of black down the centre of the belly. **Habitat**: Ranges from cultivated lands to scrub and true deserts. **Status**: Common. Occurs mostly in small flocks when not breeding. **Voice**: Sharp 'chuk chuk' given in flight. (Grysruglewerik)

12–13 cm | **Br**: Jan–Dec | J F M A M J J A S O N D

Spike-heeled Lark   NE

This small lark has an upright stance on long legs, and a long, slightly decurved bill. Its remarkably short tail is black underneath and has a contrasting white tip that is very noticeable in flight. The plumage varies from region to region but in general the bird shows buffish underparts that contrast with a white throat. **Habitat**: Wide range, from moist grassland through Karoo shrubland and semi-desert to gravel plains. **Status**: Common; almost invariably in small groups; one bird often stands sentry on low bush. **Voice**: Trilling 'trrrep, trrrep, trrrep'. (Vlaktelewerik)

43–45 cm | **Br**: Jan–Dec | J F M A M J J A S O N D

Fork-tailed Drongo

A conspicuous, noisy bird that perches freely in the open from where it hawks insects in flight or drops to the ground to retrieve food. Has a deeply forked tail and appears black all over, but in flight the underwing primaries can reflect light and wing then appears pale edged. It frequently chases buzzards and even eagles, dive-bombing them from great heights. **Habitat**: Woodland, savanna and plantations. **Status**: Common; often in pairs. **Voice**: Variety of grating or shrill notes; mimics birds of prey, especially Pearl-spotted Owlet. (Mikstertbyvanger)

23–26 cm | **Br**: Aug–Jan | J F M A M J J A S O N D

Black Cuckooshrike

Male is an all-black, slightly glossy bird with an inconspicuous yellow gape and a more obvious yellow shoulder, although the latter feature is not always present. Female is very different, resembling a female cuckoo with her green-and-yellow barred plumage, but is larger and has bright yellow outer-tail feathers. Unlike flycatchers and drongos, this bird creeps through foliage, gleaning insects from the undersides of leaves. **Habitat**: Coastal forest to bushveld. **Status**: Locally common resident and local migrant. **Voice**: High-pitched, prolonged 'trrrrrrr'. (Swartkatakoeroe)

18–21 cm | **Br: Sep–Jan** | J F M A M J J A S O N D

Ashy Tit E

This small bird has a slate-grey body, white-fringed wings, a black cap, white cheeks, and a black throat and bib extending as a black line down the belly. Very active; continually on the move through thickets, pecking and probing for food and regularly hanging upside down. Occasionally feeds on the ground where it hops about with a very upright stance. It travels in pairs or small parties, keeping in contact with a variety of ringing calls. **Habitat**: Thornveld and arid savanna. **Status**: Common. **Voice**: Harsher and more scolding than Grey Tit's. (Akasiagrysmees)

13 cm | **Br: Sep–Mar** | J F M A M J J A S O N D

Grey Tit E

Very similar to Ashy Tit but differs chiefly by having a brownish, not bluish-grey back and has buffier, not grey underparts. Their ranges do not overlap so they are unlikely to occur together, thereby ruling out confusion. Juv. is a duller version of ad. **Habitat**: Fynbos and Karoo scrub; often near rocky outcrops and old buildings. **Status**: Common; usually in small groups. **Voice**: Song is ringing, whistled 'klee-klee-klee-cheree-cheree'; harsh 'chrrr' alarm call. (Piet-tjou-tjougrysmees)

13 cm | **Br: Jul–Mar** | J F M A M J J A S O N D

Southern Black Tit

A small, strikingly marked black-and-white bird. Male is a dark sooty-black with a bold white flash across the shoulder and over the wing coverts and white-barred undertail. Female is similar to male but is paler with greyer underparts, especially on the belly and vent. Juv. is similar to female. **Habitat**: Forest and broad-leaved woodland. **Status**: Common; usually in small groups. **Voice**: Harsh, chattering 'chrr-chrr-chrr'; musical 'phee-cher-phee-cher'. (Gewone swartmees)

14–16 cm | **Br: Oct–Jan** | J F M A M J J A S O N D

Cape Crow

The only all-black crow likely to be seen in the veld, far from human habitation. The slightly decurved bill is longer and more pointed than that of any other crow. At close range it can be seen that the plumage coloration ranges from oily black to glossy deep blues and purples. Pairs are usually seen aloft man-made structures, calling to each other and flicking their wings. **Habitat**: Grassland, open country, cultivated fields and dry, desert regions. **Status**: Common; sometimes in larger flocks. **Voice**: Deep, cawing, 'kaah-kaah'; astonishing variety of bubbling calls. (Swartkraai)

43–45 cm | **Br**: Jul–Jan   J F M A M J J A S O N D

House Crow

A common and ever-increasing bird in Durban and Cape Town, where it occurs in close association with the larger Pied Crow. Easily identified by its long, thin body and tail, dark grey body and black face, wings and tail. A general scavenger in suburbia in coastal cities, occurring in small flocks but forming large roosts in trees in the evenings. **Habitat**: Usually near human habitation, where it scavenges food scraps. **Status**: Common; invader from Asia, with populations scattered along E and S coasts. **Voice**: Hurried, high-pitched 'kah, kah'. (Huiskraai)

34–38 cm | **Br**: Oct–Jan   J F M A M J J A S O N D

Pied Crow

Unmistakable: the only crow in the region to have a white belly. Could possibly be confused with the White-necked Raven when seen in flight at long range but this species has a longer tail and a smaller, more compact head. Seldom seen in flocks unless attending a kill in a game reserve or roosting in trees near cities. **Habitat**: Virtually all except driest desert areas. **Status**: Common and widespread; roosts in flocks in urban areas. **Voice**: Loud 'kwaaa' or 'kwooork' cawing. (Witborskraai)

46–50 cm | **Br**: Jul–Jan   J F M A M J J A S O N D

White-necked Raven

When seen at close range, the massive black bill with a white tip and the white crescent on the nape are diagnostic. In flight it is distinguished from other crows by its shape: large, heavy head, broad wings and a short, broad tail. Very aerodynamic, they often ride air currents in mountainous terrain, twisting and diving or chasing one another. **Habitat**: Restricted to mountainous and hilly areas. **Status**: Locally common. **Voice**: Deep, throaty 'kwaak'. (Withalskraai)

54–56 cm | **Br**: Jul–Nov   J F M A M J J A S O N D

Black-headed Oriole

A bright, golden-yellow bird with black head and throat, black wings patched with white and bright coral-red bill. Females similar to males; imm. differs by having brownish head streaked with yellow and dull red bill. Although bright, remains well concealed in the leafy canopy. Difficult to detect unless fluty song or harsher 'kweer' note is heard. **Habitat:** Mature woodland, especially broad-leaved; also forest edge and alien plantations. **Status:** Common. **Voice:** Song is explosive, whistled 'pooodleeoo'; harsher 'kweeer' note. (Swartkopwielewaal)

20–22 cm | Br: Sep–Feb   J F M A M J J A S O N D

Arrow-marked Babbler

A familiar bird in many parts of the region. Habitually travels in groups, with members of the flock following one another, either feeding on the ground or flying up to trees. The birds keep up a constant soft chatter; however, if something alarms them, the chatter builds into a crescendo. Larger than a bulbul, this babbler appears generally drab brown but at close range the arrow-like white markings down the throat and breast and the pale eye are visible. **Habitat:** Woodland and savanna. **Status:** Common. **Voice:** Noisy; raucous 'chow-chow-chow-chow...'. (Pylvlekkatlagter)

21–24 cm | Br: Jan–Dec   J F M A M J J A S O N D

Southern Pied Babbler   NE

Unmistakable. The only babbler to show a gleaming white head, back and body that contrasts with black wings and tail. Juv. is all brown initially but goes through various mottled white, rufous and brown plumages when aging. Very conspicuous when seen flying in small groups from bush to bush. **Habitat:** Arid savanna, especially acacia thornveld. **Status:** Common; occurs in groups. **Voice:** High-pitched 'kwee kwee kwee kweer' babbling. (Witkatlagter)

22–24 cm | Br: Aug–Apr   J F M A M J J A S O N D

Cape Bulbul   E

Unlikely to be mistaken for the Dark-capped or African Red-eyed bulbuls as the ranges do not overlap, and this species is easily identified by its conspicuous white eye wattle. It is also a much darker bird, having the dark head colour extending well onto the breast and belly. Is less confiding and not as habituated to man as other bulbuls. **Habitat:** Fynbos, coastal scrub and gardens. **Status:** Common. **Voice:** Song is liquid whistle, 'peet-purt-pater-ta', higher pitched and sharper than Dark-capped Bulbul's. (Kaapse tiptol)

19–21 cm | Br: Aug–Mar   J F M A M J J A S O N D

African Red-eyed Bulbul NE

Easily distinguished from the Cape and Dark-capped bulbuls by its diagnostic red eye wattle. Other less obvious differences are a darker head and an overall slightly paler appearance. The ranges of these three bulbuls rarely overlap; this species is found in the more arid regions where it is a common bird around waterholes. Hybridises with Dark-capped and Cape bulbuls in a narrow zone near Grahamstown. **Habitat**: Arid savanna, riverine bush and gardens. **Status**: Common. **Voice**: Liquid whistles, slightly flutier than Dark-capped Bulbul's. (Rooioogtiptol)

19–21 cm | Br: Sep–Apr | J F M A M J J A S O N D

Dark-capped Bulbul

One of the most familiar birds in most parts of the region as it has adapted to cities and towns and commonly frequents gardens. Has a soft, unfeathered black wattle around each eye. This distinguishes it from the African Red-eyed Bulbul, which has a red wattle. The more obvious features shared by these bulbuls are the black head and bright yellow undertail coverts. **Habitat**: Catholic, ranging from savanna to forest edge and gardens. **Status**: Abundant. **Voice**: Harsh 'kwit, kwit, kwit' alarm call; song is liquid 'sweet sweet sweet-potato'. (Swartoogtiptol)

19–22 cm | Br: Aug–Apr | J F M A M J J A S O N D

Terrestrial Brownbul

A drab, ground-dwelling forest bird lacking in any obvious diagnostic characters. Overall brownish above, slightly greyer below with a white throat. Its behaviour is a clue to its identity when small groups forage noisily on the forest floor, tossing and scattering leaf litter with their bills and feet. **Habitat**: Forest understorey and thickets. **Status**: Common; in small, noisy flocks, scuffling around on forest floor. **Voice**: Soft, chattering 'trrup cherrup trrup'. (Boskrapper)

17–19 cm | Br: Oct–Apr | J F M A M J J A S O N D

Sombre Greenbul

A very drab, olive-green bird lacking any obvious plumage diagnostic characters. At close range the white eye is diagnostic on this greenbul. Birds in the NE have contrasting yellow underparts and might be confused with the larger Yellow-bellied Greenbul but the white, not reddish eye should rule out confusion. **Habitat**: Forest and thicket; in canopy and mid-strata. **Status**: Common. **Voice**: Song is a piercing 'weeewee', usually followed by a liquid chortle, rendered 'WILLIE, quickly run around the bush and squeeeeeze-me'. (Gewone willie)

15–18 cm | Br: Sep–Dec | J F M A M J J A S O N D

Yellow-bellied Greenbul
Larger than similar Sombre Greenbul and differs chiefly by its reddish, not white eye, contrasting yellow underparts and a brownish tinge to crown and pale eye-ring. In the NE where Sombre Greenbul has yellow underparts, the reddish, not white eye and larger size help separate them. Shows bright yellow underwings in flight. **Habitat**: Thickets, dense woodland and forest edge. **Status**: Common. **Voice**: Monotonous, nasal 'nehr-nehr-nehr-nehr'; 'kwoar-tooarr' call. (Geelborswillie)

20–23 cm | **Br:** Apr–Jun   J F M A M J J A S O N D

Olive Thrush
In many respects the Olive Thrush is very similar to the Kurrichane Thrush but it has a yellow bill, a dusky speckled throat and lacks the black moustachial stripes. Forages in leaf litter but it will also take berries and fruit. **Habitat**: Forests, parks, gardens and plantations. **Status**: Common. **Voice**: Sharp 'chink' or thin 'tseeep' call; song is composed of repeated short phrases, 'wheeet-tooo-wheeet'. (Olyflyster)

20–22 cm | **Br:** Jan–Dec   J F M A M J J A S O N D

Kurrichane Thrush
Often shy in its natural environment, this bird has adapted to parks and gardens in many areas and become bold, venturing out onto open lawns in search of food. When disturbed it will fly up into a tree and sit motionless until the intruder has passed. It closely resembles the Olive Thrush but has a bright orange bill and a speckled white throat with obvious black moustachial stripes. **Habitat**: Woodland, especially miombo, and parks and gardens. **Status**: Common. **Voice**: Loud, whistling 'peet-peeoo'. (Rooibeklyster)

18–22 cm | **Br:** Aug–Mar   J F M A M J J A S O N D

Groundscraper Thrush
Frequently seen hopping around in parks and gardens and at picnic sites in game reserves. When foraging on the ground it often raises a wing, as if saluting, revealing a contrasting black-and-white pattern on the underwing. Has a very upright stance and this, combined with the bold facial markings and the heavily spotted breast, makes identification easy. **Habitat**: Found in dry thornveld, open, broad-leaved woodland, montane grassland and parks and gardens. **Status**: Common. **Voice**: Series of slow notes, 'lit-sit-si-rupa'; also clicking call. (Gevlekte lyster)

22–24 cm | **Br:** Aug–Mar   J F M A M J J A S O N D

Cape Rock-Thrush   E

A fairly shy and unobtrusive bird of rocky hillsides, it sometimes ventures into picnic sites where it becomes bold, picking up food scraps. Male is easily identified by his entirely blue head, which contrasts with the orange breast. Female is duller, being a rusty red on the head and body. Male often perches on a rock or boulder, with the bill pointing skywards, and gives his soft whistled song. **Habitat**: Rocky areas in grassland and heaths. **Status**: Common. **Voice**: Song is far-carrying, 'tsee-tseu-tseet chweeeoo' whistle; alarm is harsh grating. (Kaapse kliplyster)

19–21 cm | **Br:** Sep–Feb   J F M A M J J A S O N D

Sentinel Rock-Thrush   E

Smaller and slimmer than Cape Rock-Thrush and differs in male by having paler blue extend over the shoulders and back and further onto the throat and upper breast. Differs from male Short-toed Rock-Thrush by lacking white or pale blue forehead and crown. Female differs from female Cape Rock-Thrush by having paler underparts and smaller size. **Habitat**: Rocky terrain, usually in grassland or short heaths. **Status**: Locally common resident. **Voice**: Whistled song similar to that of Cape Rock-Thrush but more varied and not as loud. (Langtoonkliplyster)

16–18 cm | **Br:** Sep–Jan   J F M A M J J A S O N D

Short-toed Rock-Thrush   NE

Differs from both Cape and Sentinel rock-thrushes by having an obvious very pale blue or white forehead and crown. Some males have all-blue head and then told from similar male Sentinel Rock-Thrush by having a much longer and thinner bill and having a deeper blue head coloration. Female differs from similar Sentinel Rock-Thrush by having a spotted throat and orangey underparts. **Habitat**: Rocky outcrops, often with some bushes; usually in more arid areas than other rock-thrushes. **Status**: Common. **Voice**: Thin 'tseeep'; song of whistled phrases. (Korttoonkliplyster)

16–18 cm | **Br:** Aug–Mar   J F M A M J J A S O N D

African Stonechat

A small chat, the male of which has conspicuous plumage of a black head, bright white sides to the neck, a rufous chest, white patches in the wings and a white rump, all of which are very obvious in flight. Female is far drabber, lacking the black head and having rusty brown plumage, but she also shows a white rump. **Habitat**: Grassland and open areas with short scrub; also wetland areas. **Status**: Common resident with some local movements. **Voice**: A 'weeet' followed by a harsh 'chaaak'. (Gewone bontrokkie)

13–14 cm | **Br:** Jul–Jan   J F M A M J J A S O N D

Familiar Chat

A small, dark greyish-brown bird that lacks any obvious field characters except its behaviour. Most small chats have the habit of nervously flicking their wings slightly open, which exposes the normally boldly-patterned rump and uppertail: the Familiar Chat continually performs this wing-flicking motion, and displays a russet rump and outer-tail feathers. **Habitat**: It inhabits rocky and mountainous terrain, and open woodland in some areas. **Status**: Common. **Voice**: Harsh, scolding 'shek-shek' alarm call; warbling trill. (Gewone spekvreter)

14–15 cm | Br: Jul–Apr | J F M A M J J A S O N D

Sickle-winged Chat   E

Resembles mostly Familiar Chat but differs by being paler, especially on the underparts. The rump and sides to tail are buff and not the rich chestnut of Familiar Chat and its legs are longer and much thinner. In further comparison to Familiar Chat it spends more time foraging on the ground, where it runs more swiftly. **Habitat**: Grassland, taller Karoo scrub and fields. **Status**: Locally common. **Voice**: Very soft, typically chat-like 'chak-chak'; warbled song. (Vlaktespekvreter)

14–15 cm | Br: Aug–Mar | J F M A M J J A S O N D

juv.

Karoo Chat   NE

Could be confused with similar all-grey form of the Mountain Wheatear but has a dark, not white rump and has all-white outer-tail feathers. Differs from both Tractrac and Sickle-winged chats by being larger and lacking white or buff on the rump. Birds in the NW are very much paler. **Habitat**: Grassland, taller Karoo scrub and fields. **Status**: Locally common. **Voice**: Very soft, typically chat-like 'chak-chak'; warbled song. (Karoospekvreter)

16–18 cm | Br: Aug–Mar | J F M A M J J A S O N D

Tractrac Chat   NE

Differs from similar Sickle-winged and Familiar chats by being overall paler and has a white rump and sides to the tail's base. Smaller than Karoo Chat and lacks that species' dark rump and total white outer-tail feathers. Birds in coastal Namibia are almost totally white with darker wings and tail. **Habitat**: Karoo and desert scrub, hummock dunes and gravel plains. **Status**: Common; usually in pairs or family groups. **Voice**: Soft, fast 'tactac'; song is quiet, musical bubbling; territorial defence call is loud chattering. (Woestynspekvreter)

14–15 cm | Br: Aug–Apr | J F M A M J J A S O N D

Mountain Wheatear   NE

When driving over mountain passes or through rocky, arid areas, the startling black-and-white bird that flushes from the roadside is most likely to be this species. Very flighty and nervous, it will not allow close approach but the very obvious black-and-white pied plumage should render it unmistakable. Some males are greyish instead of black but all show a white cap, shoulder patch and rump. Female is greyish and nondescript but also shows diagnostic white rump. **Habitat**: Rocky hillsides and boulders. **Status**: Common. **Voice**: Clear, thrush-like whistling. (Bergwagter)

18–20 cm | Br: Sep–Feb   J F M A M J J A S O N D

Capped Wheatear

A bird of open, level veld with little grass cover and plenty of termite mounds to use as look-out posts. It has a very upright posture at rest. It can run very rapidly and, when it flies, its white rump and sides of the tail are conspicuous. The white eyebrow stripe, black cap and black collar are diagnostic. **Habitat**: Barren, sandy or stony areas and short grassland in flat country. **Status**: Common resident with local movements. **Voice**: 'Chik-chik' alarm note; song is loud warbling with slurred chattering. (Hoëveldskaapwagter)

17–18 cm | Br: Jul–Jan   J F M A M J J A S O N D

Cape Rockjumper   E

Confusable only with Drakensberg Rock-jumper but they are confined to different areas so would never be seen together, thereby avoiding confusion. Male has a deep rusty breast and belly and male of Drakensberg Rock-jumper has a pale orangey-yellow belly. Female Drakensberg Rock-jumper is overall very much paler than female Cape Rock-jumper. **Habitat**: Rocky mountain slopes and scree. **Status**: Common but localised; usually in small groups. **Voice**: Series of loud, high-pitched whistles. (Kaapse berglyster)

23–25 cm | Br: Jul–Jan   J F M A M J J A S O N D

Drakensberg Rockjumper E

Separated by being paler overall than Cape Rock-jumper, especially on the breast and belly. This species is confined to the Drakensberg Massif and is not known from the Cape mountains further S, so confusion is hardly likely. Female is much paler than female Cape Rock-jumper. **Habitat**: Usually above 2 000 m on rocky slopes. **Status**: Locally common; usually in small groups. **Voice**: Rapidly repeated, piping whistles, like Cape Rock-jumper's. (Oranjeborsberglyster)

23–25 cm | Br: Aug–Feb   J F M A M J J A S O N D

Buff-streaked Chat   E

Male of this small chat is distinctive and its black face, buff scapulars and black wings are all diagnostic. Its white eyebrow stripe connects to the characteristic buffy 'V' scapulars down the sides of the head. Female resembles juv. Capped Wheatear but has a buff, not white rump. Juv. is a mottled version of female. **Habitat**: Rock-strewn, grassy slopes. **Status**: Common but localised. **Voice**: Loud, rich warbling, including mimicry of other birds' songs. (Bergklipwagter)

16–17 cm | **Br**: Sep–Feb   J F M A M J J A S O N D   ♀

Ant-eating Chat

Always occurs in pairs or small parties and is very active, taking short flights, hopping across the veld or hovering into the wind before darting off downwind. Appears black but at close range its rich chocolate-brown plumage can be seen. Some males have a white shoulder patch but all birds show white 'windows' in the wing tips, a feature visible only in flight. **Habitat**: Grassland dotted with termite mounds, and open, sandy or stony areas. **Status**: Common. **Voice**: Short, sharp 'peek' or 'piek' call; song is varied mix of whistles and grating notes. (Swartpiek)

17–18 cm | **Br**: Aug–Mar   J F M A M J J A S O N D

Mocking Cliff Chat

A black-and-chestnut bird of wooded gullies and cliffs. Male's black head, back, wings and breast contrast with the rich chestnut lower underparts and rump. Shows a distinct white shoulder patch and a more obscure white line separating black breast band with chestnut belly. Female similar to male but has the black replaced with dark grey and lacks any white in the plumage. **Habitat**: Bases of cliffs and wooded, rocky slopes. **Status**: Common but localised; usually in pairs or family parties. **Voice**: Loud, melodious, whistled song, often with much mimicry. (Dassievoël)

19–21 cm | **Br**: Aug–Dec   J F M A M J J A S O N D

Chorister Robin-Chat   E

Most likely to be confused with Red-capped Robin Chat but is overall much darker and has dark, not powder-blue shoulders and has a black, not orangey-red face. Leg colour also differs in being fleshy pink, not dark. Hybridisation occurs between the two species but is rare. **Habitat**: Forest and coastal thickets. **Status**: Common resident with local movements from interior to coastal forests in winter. **Voice**: Contact call is plaintive 'toy-toy, toy-toy'; song is loud and bubbly, including much mimicry of other forest birds. (Lawaaimakerjanfrederik)

20 cm | **Br**: Oct–Dec   J F M A M J J A S O N D

Red-capped Robin-Chat

This small forest robin is extremely shy and furtive, preferring to keep to the darker tangles of thickets in evergreen forests where, during the day, it forages in leaf litter. At dusk and dawn it becomes more confident and will enter open areas at the forest edge to feed. The bright orange-red plumage with powder-blue wings is diagnostic. **Habitat**: Thickets and tangles in forest and dense woodland. **Status**: Common. **Voice**: Call is soft, slightly trilled 'seee-saw', often repeated; song is rambling series of melodious whistles, including much mimicry. (Nataljanfrederik)

16–18 cm | **Br: Sep–Jan** | J F M A M J J A S O N D

Cape Robin-Chat

Easily recognised by its short, white eyebrow stripe and by having the orange coloration confined to the throat and upper breast. Feeds mostly on the ground but creeps up through vegetation and sits on an exposed perch to sing. Imm. is mottled and spotted buff but shows a reddish tail with a dark centre. **Habitat**: Wide range: forest edge, thickets, heaths, scrub, gardens and parks; occurs at higher elevations in N, but common at sea level in S. **Status**: Common. **Voice**: Song is series of melodious phrases. (Gewone janfrederik)

16–17 cm | **Br: Jun–Mar** | J F M A M J J A S O N D

White-browed Robin-Chat

An explosive rush of melodious and repetitive song from thick, tangled scrub early in the morning often indicates the presence of this species. It is furtive but, if seen, the red-orange underparts and dark head with a broad, white eyebrow stripe soon identify this bird. Imm. is drabber than the ad. and has buff-tipped feathers on the mantle and back. **Habitat**: Dense thickets and tangles, gardens and parks. **Status**: Common. **Voice**: Characteristic, loud, crescendo song of repeated phrases; also is accomplished mimic. (Heuglinjanfrederik)

19–20 cm | **Br: Aug–Jan** | J F M A M J J A S O N D

White-throated Robin-Chat   E

The very obvious white wing bar, white throat and breast and rusty flanks are diagnostic on this small robin-chat. If seen from behind with tail partially spread, the dark-centred rufous tail also has a dark tip, which is unique in local robin-chats. **Habitat**: Thickets and riverine scrub in woodland and savanna; usually feeds on ground, but sings from elevated perches. **Status**: Common. **Voice**: Alarm call is repeated 'seet-cher, seet-cher'; song is rather short series of rich whistles; often mimics other birds. (Witkeeljanfrederik)

17 cm | **Br: Sep–Jan** | J F M A M J J A S O N D

White-browed Scrub Robin

The bird has diagnostic heavy streaking down the breast, a white eyebrow stripe and white spots in the wing that form a white wing bar. The tail tip is spotted white; the tail is frequently raised and lowered, displaying the russet rump. **Habitat**: Found in both dry and moist broad-leaved woodland, thornveld and forest. **Status**: Common. **Voice**: Harsh 'trrrrr' alarm note; fluty but repetitive song; characteristic call at dawn and dusk is a whistled 'seep po go'. (Gestreepte wipstert)

14–16 cm | Br: Sep–Jan | J F M A M J J A S O N D

Kalahari Scrub Robin   NE

Similar to White-browed Scrub-Robin but has plain, not streaked underparts and has much more rufous on rump and tail. Differs further by lacking the double white wing bar. In N Namibia White-browed Scrub-Robin lacks breast streaking, which could cause confusion with this species but differs by lacking white wing bars and has more rufous on tail. **Habitat**: Dry acacia savanna. **Status**: Common. **Voice**: Alarm note is harsh 'zzeee'; contact call is whistled 'seeeup'; musical song of whistles and chirps. (Kalahariwipstert)

14–16 cm | Br: Jul–Jan | J F M A M J J A S O N D

Karoo Scrub Robin   E

This small greyish bird is common in the fynbos of the S and W and in the more arid regions. It is easily recognised if flushed as the black tail, which is held fanned in flight, shows a conspicuous white tip. The overall plumage is drab grey, slightly paler below, and there is a short white eyebrow stripe and a russet base to the tail. **Habitat**: Frequents semi-arid scrub and fynbos. **Status**: Common; usually in pairs. **Voice**: Harsh chattering 'chik chik tcheet'; song is a mixture of whistles and harsh grating notes. (Slangverklikker)

14–17 cm | Br: Jul–Dec | J F M A M J J A S O N D

Bearded Scrub Robin

A small bird with brown upperparts. Black-edged, white eyebrow stripe, black malar stripes, buffy orange flanks and upper breast and rufous rump are diagnostic. Juv. is mottled with tawny buff; tail is the same as that of ad. **Habitat**: Dry forest, broad-leaved woodland and thornveld. **Status**: Common resident. **Voice**: Alarm call is sharp notes followed by 'churr, chek-chek kwezzz'; song is clear, consisting of often-repeated, mixed phrases. (Baardwipstert)

14–17 cm | Br: Sep–Dec | J F M A M J J A S O N D

Willow Warbler

A small, sometimes very common migrant warbler. Variable in colour from greyish birds showing little yellow on the underparts to very bright green birds with bright yellow underparts. Juv. usually brighter yellow on the underparts than ad. and has greener upperparts. Very vocal and most often detected by its song and soft contact notes. **Habitat:** Wide range of woodland and savanna. **Status:** Abundant Palaearctic migrant Oct–May. **Voice:** Soft, two-note contact call, 'hoeet hoeet'; short, melodious song, descending in scale. (Hofsanger)

11 cm | Br: n/a J F M A M J J A S O N D

Yellow-bellied Eremomela

A small grey warbler with yellow-washed belly and vent. Yellow on the underparts vary greatly from bright to a faint wash on the belly and flanks. Larger than Cape Penduline -it and has a longer tail, longer, thinner bill and lacks the black-speckled forehead. The dark eye-stripe through the brown eye contrasts with the pale grey eyebrow stripe. **Habitat:** Semi-arid savanna, broad-leaved woodland and scrub. **Status:** Common; usually solitary or in pairs. **Voice:** Song is crombec-like: high-pitched, frequently repeated 'tchee-tchee-tchee'. (Geelpensbossanger)

10 cm | Br: Aug–May J F M A M J J A S O N D

Cape Penduline-Tit   NE

A minute grey and yellowish bird. Might be confused with eremomelas but is smaller (the region's smallest bird), has a more conical bill, rotund body shape and shorter tail. The black-speckled forehead differentiates it from Yellow-bellied Eremomela. Juv. has paler underparts than ad. **Habitat:** Fynbos, Karoo scrub, semi-desert and arid savanna. **Status:** Common. **Voice:** Soft, high-pitched 'tseep' or 'tsip-eep-eep'. (Kaapse kapokvoël)

8 cm | Br: Jun–Apr J F M A M J J A S O N D

Grey Penduline-Tit

This small bird differs from Cape Penduline-Tit by lacking that species' black forehead, eye-stripe and speckled throat. It further differs in being greyer, with buff underparts, whitish breast and buff forehead and face. **Habitat:** Broad-leaved and miombo woodlands. **Status:** Common resident. **Voice:** Call is a soft 'chissick' or 'tseeep'. (Gryskapokvoël)

8 cm | Br: Aug–Feb J F M A M J J A S O N D

Little Rush Warbler

Much darker brown than other reed-dwelling warblers, with mottled throat and breast and a long, broad tail. When breeding has a distinctive display flight just above reeds on fluttering wings as it gives its ratchet-like call. **Habitat**: Reeds and sedges, usually in denser areas further from water than reed-warblers. **Status**: Locally common resident with local movements. **Voice**: Harsh, ratchet-like 'brrrup... brrrup... trrp... trrp... trrp' song, accelerating towards the end and usually accompanied by a wing rattle; also nasal 'wheeaaa'. (Kaapse vleisanger)

13–16 cm | **Br**: Sep–Mar   J F M A M J J A S O N D

Lesser Swamp Warbler

Resembles mostly the African Reed-Warbler, from which it is best told apart by its larger size, with clearer white underparts, and a much whiter face with well-defined white eyebrow stripe. This species is the most visible of the reed-dwelling warblers, often seen sitting exposed in the open stretches of reeds over water. **Habitat**: Reed beds, usually over water. **Status**: Common; easily observed, often foraging in the open. **Voice**: Rich, fluty 'cheerup-chee-chiree-chiree' song. (Kaapse rietsanger)

14–16 cm | **Br**: Jul–May   J F M A M J J A S O N D

African Reed Warbler

Differs from Lesser Swamp-Warbler by being smaller and much buffier on vent, flanks and belly. Very much smaller than Great Reed-Warbler and has a much thinner, shorter bill. Juv. resembles ad. but has a bright rufous rump. **Habitat**: Over or very close to marshy ground in reed or sedge beds or in rank, reedy areas. **Status**: Common summer visitor. **Voice**: A jumbled song that includes mimicry of other birds. (Kleinrietsanger)

12–13 cm | **Br**: Sep–Jan   J F M A M J J A S O N D

Great Reed Warbler

A very large reed-dwelling warbler. It most closely resembles in colour the African Reed-Warbler but is larger, has a longer, more robust bill, and a well-defined pale eyebrow stripe. It further differs by having pale greyish, not dark legs. Most often detected by its harsh, guttural song. **Habitat**: Reed beds and bush thickets; often near water. **Status**: Common Palaearctic migrant Oct–Apr. **Voice**: Prolonged, rambling 'chee-chee-chaak-chaak-chuk-chuk' song, slower than those of smaller reed-warblers. (Grootrietsanger)

18–20 cm | **Br**: n/a   J F M A M J J A S O N D

Sedge Warbler

The most obvious feature of this small reed-dwelling migrant warbler is the heavily streaked crown and contrasting broad white eyebrow stripe. The back is also well streaked and the underparts are buff with warmer flanks. Superficially resembles a cisticola but the white eyebrow stripe and lack of a long tail with black-and-white tip should rule out confusion. **Habitat**: Reed beds and rank weedy areas bordering wetlands, and thickets sometimes far from water. **Status**: Common Palaearctic migrant. **Voice**: Harsh chattering. (Europese vleisanger)

12–13 cm | Br: n/a   J F M A M J J A S O N D

Cape Grassbird   E

Resembles a cisticola but is very much larger. The combination of the long, straggly tail, bright chestnut cap and black moustachial and malar stripes is diagnostic. Often flushed from long grass when the long, pointed tail is obvious and appears worn and tatty. **Habitat**: Fynbos and rank grass on mountain slopes and near water. **Status**: Common; mostly remains in dense vegetation, but easily located by song. **Voice**: Soft series of warbling notes, building in volume, pace and pitch, then ending with loud 'wheeeooo'; nasal 'where' call. (Grasvoël)

17–19 cm | Br: Jul–Apr   J F M A M J J A S O N D

Green-backed Camaroptera

This species resembles the well-known Wren of the northern hemisphere. It keeps low down in thick vegetation and habitually cocks its tail. It has off-white to greyish underparts. When excited or disturbed, it will flit through the undergrowth giving a metallic clicking sound. **Habitat**: Dense undergrowth and tangles in forest and thickets. **Status**: Common. **Voice**: Similar to that of Grey-backed Camaroptera, but the normal call is a loud, snapping 'bidup-bidup-bidup'. (Groenrugkwêkwêvoël)

10–11 cm | Br: Sep–Apr   J F M A M J J A S O N D

Grey-backed Camaroptera

Identical to Green-backed Camaroptera except this species has a greyish, not olive-green back and greyish head and throat when breeding. In non-br. plumage the back is an ashy-brown colour. A small, rotund warbler that habitually cocks its tail and, when excited, snaps its wings. **Habitat**: Dense vegetation in woodland, thicket and forest, including gardens; usually remains in understorey or mid-strata. **Status**: Common. **Voice**: Often repeated, nasal 'neeehhh' (resulting in common name, 'bleating warbler'); loud, snapping 'bidup-bidup-bidup'. (Grysrugkwêkwêvoël)

10–11 cm | Br: Sep–Apr   J F M A M J J A S O N D

Fairy Flycatcher E

A small, dainty bird with more warbler-like habits than a flycatcher. The delicate pinkish wash across the breast combined with the black mask, white stripe across the wing and white outer-tail feathers are all diagnostic. Juv. is more brownish than ad. Active and lively as it creeps through foliage where it gleans insects. **Habitat:** Karoo scrub and montane heath in summer, dispersing down to acacia savanna in winter. **Status:** Common resident and altitudinal migrant. **Voice:** Wispy, high-pitched 'tisee-tchee-tchee'; descending 'cher cher cher'. (Feevlieëvanger)

12 cm | **Br:** Jul–Dec | J F M A M J J A S O N D

Chestnut-vented Tit-Babbler

Most often seen as it creeps through thick thornbush delivering its loud, explosive song. It is a greyish bird with a longish tail, chestnut vent (diagnostic), and a pale eye. The folded wing shows a chequered shoulder and the throat is streaked black. Occurs mostly in pairs, which maintain contact through their fluty calls. **Habitat:** Inhabits dry thornveld, thickets and dry scrub in arid regions. **Status:** Common. **Voice:** The song is rendered as a liquid 'cheruuup-chee-chee', interspersed with harsher, chattering notes. (Bosveldtjeriktik)

14–15 cm | **Br:** Jul–Apr | J F M A M J J A S O N D

Long-billed Crombec

A small, greyish bird with buffy cinnamon underparts, this species appears almost tailless. It is easily distinguished from similar warblers as the bill is long and noticeably decurved. This active bird occurs in pairs or small groups and is a regular attendant at bird parties. It feeds by gleaning insects from branches and leaves and will probe crevices with its long bill. **Habitat:** Occurs in a wide range of woodlands and semi-arid scrub; avoids moist forests. **Status:** Common. **Voice:** Song is loud, repeated 'tree-rriit, trree-rriit' or 'trree reee rit' whistle. (Bosveldstompstert)

12 cm | **Br:** Aug–Mar | J F M A M J J A S O N D

Yellow-breasted Apalis

Apalises are lively, long-tailed warblers, continually on the move in forest or bush and, although many of them remain high in the canopy, this species prefers the lower or mid-stratum. It can be identified by the combination of a greyish cap, white throat and bright yellow breast, which, in the male, has a small black bar on the lower breast. **Habitat:** Woodland, dense savanna and thickets; avoids montane forest. **Status:** Common. **Voice:** Fast, buzzy 'chizzick-chizzick-chizzick'; pairs often duet. (Geelborskleinjantjie)

11–12 cm | **Br:** May–Jun, Oct–Feb | J F M A M J J A S O N D

Bar-throated Apalis

This small, long-tailed bird is easily identified by its greyish or greenish upperparts, creamy underparts with a thin, dark bar across the breast and a pale, creamy eye. Might be mistaken for Yellow-breasted Apalis but lacks any yellow on the breast. Occurs in pairs in forest or scrub and creeps through the mid-stratum or low down, gleaning insects or caterpillars from under leaves. **Habitat**: Forest, dense woodland and coastal thickets. Restricted to montane forest in N of range. **Status**: Common. **Voice**: Utters harsh 'krrup-krrup-krrup'. (Bandkeelkleinjantjie)

11–12 cm | Br: Jul–Mar   J F M A M J J A S O N D

Neddicky

Occurs in two colour forms. Birds in the S have greyish underparts whereas the northern birds have dusky brown underparts. The combination of a chestnut cap, grey underparts and uniform brownish upperparts makes this small cisticola relatively easy to identify. Often cocks its tail like a camaroptera. **Habitat**: Grassy understorey of woodland and savanna; also mountain fynbos and plantations, especially where there are dead trees. **Status**: Common. **Voice**: Monotonous, high-pitched, frog-like 'tseeep tseeep tseeep'. (Neddikkie)

11 cm | Br: Sep–Mar   J F M A M J J A S O N D

Zitting Cisticola

Cisticolas are notoriously difficult to identify and the Zitting Cisticola is no exception unless the bird is calling or displaying. It is a tiny bird with a finely streaked forehead and well-marked buff and black back. The tail, which is short and often held fanned, has a dark subterminal band and a white tip. **Habitat**: Thick grass and fields, often in damp areas. **Status**: Common. **Voice**: Monotonous 'zit zit zit', repeated 1–2 times per second during display flight, 10–30 m over territory. Does not snap wings. (Landeryklopkloppie)

10 cm | Br: Aug–Apr   J F M A M J J A S O N D

Desert Cisticola

Usually found in much drier habitat than similar Zitting Cisticola. Very difficult to tell apart from Zitting Cisticola unless singing but at close range the lack of a black tip to the tail is a useful field character. It is also overall paler with less defined pattern on the upperparts. **Habitat**: Arid grassland and old fields. **Status**: Common. **Voice**: Song is fast 'zink zink zink', 'sii sii sii' or 'su-ink su-ink su-ink', typically faster than Zitting Cisticola's and interspersed with sharp wing-snapping. Display flight is fairly low and jerky. (Woestynklopkloppie)

10 cm | Br: Oct–Apr   J F M A M J J A S O N D

Grey-backed Cisticola   E

This bird, the common cisticola in fynbos and arid Karoo scrub, is long-tailed and has a grey-streaked back and chestnut cap. For most of the year it is unobtrusive and skulks in scrub but when breeding it becomes obvious with its aerial display and calls. **Habitat**: Lowland fynbos, Karoo scrub and arid, grassy hillsides, typically in drier habitat. **Status**: Common. **Voice**: Muffled 'tr-r-rrrrrt' and loud, plaintive 'hu-weeeee', given from perch or in air; also harsher 'chee chee' call. (Grysrugtinktinkie)

13–14 cm | Br: Jul–Feb   J F M A M J J A S O N D

Rattling Cisticola

Most abundant cisticola of the thornveld and probably the most conspicuous of all the cisticolas. Perches openly on the tops of bushes and proclaims its territory with a loud 'chureee-chureee' song that ends with a rattling 'cherrrr'. When one is walking through the bush, this is the small, long-tailed bird with a chestnut cap that approaches and boldly scolds with a consistent 'cheee-cheee' alarm note. **Habitat**: Woodland, savanna and scrub. **Status**: Common to abundant. **Voice**: Loud, scolding 'chee chee chrrrrr' or 'chee chee chee tup-up-up'. (Bosveldtinktinkie)

11–14 cm | Br: Oct–Apr   J F M A M J J A S O N D

Levaillant's Cisticola

A very brightly coloured reed-dwelling cisticola. Shows a bright chestnut cap, blackish back with feathers broadly edged with buff and brown, a rufous tail tipped with black and small rufous panel in the wings. The underparts are creamy white. In non-br. plumage the bird is duller overall. **Habitat**: Reed beds, sedges and long grass adjacent to wetlands. **Status**: Common. **Voice**: Warbling, musical 'chrip-trrrup-trrree'; wailing 'cheee-weee-weee'. (Vleitinktinkie)

14 cm | Br: Jul–Apr   J F M A M J J A S O N D

Red-faced Cisticola

Its preferred habitat of reed beds is a clue to its identity. Differs from all other reed-dwelling cisticolas by having a uniform, not streaked back. In br. plumage the face, sides of the breast and flanks are washed pale rufous. Usually seen in pairs and duet when singing. **Habitat**: Rank vegetation next to pans and streams. **Status**: Common. **Voice**: Male utters a series of piercing whistles, typically descending in pitch. Also dry 'prrt prrt' calls. Female usually calls with male, deep 'zidit'. Alarm call is thin, high-pitched 'tseeeep'. (Rooiwangtinktinkie)

13–14 cm | Br: Oct–Mar   J F M A M J J A S O N D

Rufous-eared Warbler   E

The combination of rufous ear patches and narrow black breast band is diagnostic. Very prinia-like in habits and frequently feeds on the ground and runs swiftly from bush to bush with its tail cocked. Juv. is similar to ad., but has faded breast band and dull ear patches. **Habitat**: Arid scrub and grassland with scattered bushes; often forages on ground, running swiftly from bush to bush. **Status**: Common. **Voice**: Scolding, high-pitched 'chweeo, chweeo, chweeo...'. (Rooioorlangstertjie)

14–15 cm | Br: Jul–Mar | J F M A M J J A S O N D

Karoo Prinia   E

The common prinia found in low scrub, bracken and briar habitat in fynbos, the Karoo and some mountainous areas. Unlikely to be confused with other prinias or cisticolas because of the diagnostic streaking on its breast. Like other prinias, it has a long tail that is often held cocked at right angles. **Habitat**: Fynbos, thickets and taller Karoo scrub. **Status**: Common; usually in pairs and territorial year round. **Voice**: Wide range of scolding calls, including sharp 'chleet-chleet-chleet' and faster 'tit-tit-tit-tit'. (Karoolangstertjie)

12–14 cm | Br: Jul–Mar | J F M A M J J A S O N D

Tawny-flanked Prinia

Very similar to non-br. Black-chested Prinia, but is paler below with a whitish, not creamy yellow breast and throat, warm buff breast and belly and rufous edges to wings. It is also slightly smaller and slimmer than Black-chested Prinia and has a brighter red eye. Usually found in pairs creeping through rank grass and thickets, giving their soft contact call. **Habitat**: Woodland and thick, rank vegetation. **Status**: Common. **Voice**: Rapidly repeated 'przzt-przzt-przzt'; harsh 'chrzzzt'. (Bruinsylangstertjie)

11–12 cm | Br: Jul–Apr | J F M A M J J A S O N D

Black-chested Prinia

The only prinia in the region to have a broad black breast band in br. plumage. Female's breast band is narrower. In non-br. plumage it lacks the breast band and resembles the smaller Tawny-flanked Prinia but is yellowish, not white on the throat and is more yellowish on the underparts and lacks rufous edging to the wings. **Habitat**: Arid scrub, savanna, plantations and gardens. **Status**: Common. **Voice**: Loud, repetitive 'zzzrt-zzzzrt-zzzrt-zzzrt'. (Swartbandlangstertjie)

14–15 cm | Br: Aug–Mar | J F M A M J J A S O N D

African Dusky Flycatcher
Only at close range can the lack of streaking on the forehead be seen, which distinguishes this species from the very similar Spotted Flycatcher, which has marked forehead streaking. It further differs from the Spotted Flycatcher by having more diffuse streaking on the underparts and is smaller and shorter winged. Juv. is a mottled and spotted version of ad. **Habitat**: Forest edges and glades, riverine forest and well-wooded gardens. **Status**: Common. **Voice**: Soft, high-pitched 'tzzeet' and 'tsirit'. (Donkervlieëvanger)

12 cm | Br: Sep–Apr   J F M A M J J A S O N D

Spotted Flycatcher
Confusion is most likely with African Dusky Flycatcher but differs by being larger, much longer winged and having a streaked forehead and much more clearly and paler streaked underparts. Has the unusual habit of flicking its wings on alighting. **Habitat**: Virtually all wooded habitats, from forest edges to semi-arid savanna. **Status**: Common Palaearctic migrant Oct–Apr. **Voice**: Soft 'tzee' and 'zeck, chick-chick'. (Europese vlieëvanger)

13–14 cm | Br: n/a   J F M A M J J A S O N D

Ashy Flycatcher
A small flycatcher with bluish grey upperparts, whitish underparts and a bluish breast band. The facial pattern shows pale eye-ring and whitish loral stripe and black line from bill to eye. Sits motionless for long periods and then suddenly dashes from perch to pick up flying insect or to the ground for a small invertebrate. **Habitat**: Riverine forests and moist, open broad-leaved woodland. **Status**: Common. **Voice**: Song is soft 'sszzit-sszzit-sreee-sreee', descending in scale. (Blougrysvlieëvanger)

14–15 cm | Br: Sep–Jan   J F M A M J J A S O N D

Southern Black Flycatcher
Very similar to Black Cuckooshrike, but differs in having a square-ended, not rounded tail and lacks a yellow gape and shoulder. Also differs in feeding method; this species actively chases insects in the air and the cuckooshrike gleans insects while creeping among foliage. Juv. is spotted black and brown. **Habitat**: Woodland, savanna and forest edges. **Status**: Common; sallies from perches, taking food from ground. **Voice**: Song is wheezy 'tzzit-terra-loora-loo'. (Swartvlieëvanger)

20–22 cm | Br: May, Aug–Mar   J F M A M J J A S O N D

Fiscal Flycatcher E

This bird resembles a Common Fiscal but it has a shorter tail with obvious white patches on either side, it lacks white on the shoulders and has a short, fine bill and not the thick, hooked bill of a shrike. Its habits also differ in that it behaves like a flycatcher and does not sit in such exposed situations as the Common Fiscal. Imm. is brown, not black. **Habitat**: Woodland and thickets, scrub, gardens and plantations. **Status**: Common resident, subject to local movements in winter. **Voice**: High-pitched, chittering song; 'tssisk' alarm call. (Fiskaalvlieëvanger)

17–20 cm | Br: Jul–Mar   J F M A M J J A S O N D

Chat Flycatcher

Range does not overlap with Pale Flycatcher so confusion is ruled out. Most likely to be confused with Marico Flycatcher whose range it overlaps. It differs by being very much larger and more robust and has darker, not gleaming white underparts. Shows a pale panel on the folded wing. Juv. has spotted and mottled plumage. **Habitat**: Semi-arid and arid shrublands. **Status**: Common. **Voice**: Song is rich, warbled 'cher-cher-cherrip', with squeaky, hissing notes. (Grootvlieëvanger)

20 cm | Br: Jul–May   J F M A M J J A S O N D

Marico Flycatcher

A nondescript flycatcher with uniform dun-brown upperparts and clear white underparts. At close range a buffish ring around the eye and a buff panel in the wings are discernible. At rest, the bird appears very white-breasted and has an upright stance. It uses prominent perches from which it hawks insects; it often returns to the same perch. **Habitat**: Occurs in mixed thornveld and dry, broad-leaved woodland in the drier NW regions. **Status**: Locally common; in pairs and small groups. **Voice**: Song is melodious warbling. (Maricovlieëvanger)

18 cm | Br: Jan–Dec   J F M A M J J A S O N D

Pale Flycatcher

This species and the Marico Flycatcher are very similar but Pale Flycatcher is overall much darker and lacks the gleaming white underparts. The upperparts are more greyish, less brown than in Marico Flycatcher. Juv. has a variable amount of buff spotting on the back and is sometimes heavily spotted brown on the underparts. **Habitat**: Moist, broad-leaved woodland. **Status**: Locally common. **Voice**: Song is melodious warbling interspersed with harsh chitters; alarm call is soft 'churr'. (Muiskleurvlieëvanger)

17 cm | Br: Sep–Mar   J F M A M J J A S O N D

African Paradise Flycatcher

Male is unmistakable. It has an extra-ordinarily long tail (18 cm) which, like the back, is rufous and contrasts with the blue-grey underparts and darker head. Female and imm. lack the very long tail. An active and noisy bird, whose harsh calls are often heard before the bird is seen. Dashes about in the mid-canopy chasing insects, rarely settling for long. **Habitat**: Forest and dense woodland; also gardens. **Status**: Common resident and intra-African migrant. **Voice**: Harsh 'zweet-zweet-zwayt' call; song is loud, whistled 'twee-tiddly-te-te'. (Paradysvlieëvanger)

17 20 cm | **Br: Aug–Jan** J F M A M J J A S O N D

Cape White-eye E

The plumage of this warbler-like bird varies from region to region but it is usually olive-green above, greyish below and has a diagnostic ring of white feathering around the eye. They are noisy and active birds, commonly found in groups as they work their way through the undergrowth or high canopy. They are inveterate members of bird parties. **Habitat**: Woodland, forests, thickets, plantations and gardens. **Status**: Common to abundant. **Voice**: Remarkably loud warbling song uttered mostly at dawn; also constant chittering contact calls. (Kaapse glasogie)

12 cm | **Br: Jan–Dec** J F M A M J J A S O N D

Pririt Batis NE

Most likely to be confused with Cape Batis but their ranges and habitats do not overlap, thereby avoiding confusion. Female has a pale orangey wash across the throat and breast while male's black breast can vary from broad to narrow black. **Habitat**: Acacia thickets, arid broad-leaved woodland and dry riverine bush. **Status**: Common. **Voice**: Series of numerous, slow 'teuu, teuu, teuu, teuu' notes, descending in scale, often with sharp clicking calls. (Priritbosbontrokkie)

12 cm | **Br: Aug–Nov** J F M A M J J A S O N D

Cape Batis E

A large and chunky batis. Male shows russet over the wings and flanks as well as a broad black breast band; female might be mistaken for the Chinspot Batis but has the russet breast band extending down the sides of the breast and over the flanks. It occurs in pairs and in bird parties and is an active flycatcher in the mid-canopy. **Habitat**: Forests, riparian thickets and even well-wooded gardens. **Status**: Common. **Voice**: Soft, pish-like 'shwee ksh ksh ksh ksha'; whistled 'foo-foo-foo'. (Kaapse bosbontrokkie)

13 cm | **Br: Aug–Feb** J F M A M J J A S O N D

Chinspot Batis

A small, black-and-white flycatcher, the female of which has a broad chestnut breast band and a diagnostic chestnut spot on the chin. Male lacks the chestnut spot and its breast band is black. Normally occurs in pairs. Will glean insects from foliage as well as hawk flies, which it does with an audible snap of the bill. **Habitat**: Broad-leaved woodland and acacia savanna. **Status**: Common. **Voice**: Clear, descending 2–4 whistled notes, 'teuu-teuu-teuu' ('three blind mice'); harsh 'chrr-chrr' notes. (Witliesbosbontrokkie)

13 cm | **Br**: Aug–Feb   J F M A M J J A S O N D

Cape Wagtail

A dowdier bird than the African Pied Wagtail, with the black being replaced by greyish-brown, which sometimes has an olive wash. Habits similar to those of the African Pied Wagtail, with much running around and tail wagging when chasing insects. Prefers damp and marshy areas but will frequent watered grassy lawns in parks and gardens. When not breeding, large flocks may gather to form communal roosts in trees. **Habitat**: Open grassland, usually near water, but also in gardens. **Status**: Common. **Voice**: Clear, ringing 'tseee-chee-chee'. (Gewone kwikkie)

19–20 cm | **Br**: Jan–Dec   J F M A M J J A S O N D

African Pied Wagtail

Unmistakable and unlikely to be confused with any other species in the region. The black-and-white plumage, combined with the long tail that is continually bobbed up and down, is diagnostic. Female has a sootier breast band than male. Feeds on the ground, usually in damp areas close to water, but may be found far from water. Dashes to and fro chasing insects, its tail busily moving up and down. **Habitat**: Large rivers, wetlands and coastal lagoons; also in large gardens near water. **Status**: Locally common. **Voice**: Loud, shrill 'chee-chee-cheree-cheeroo'. (Bontkwikkie)

20 cm | **Br**: Jul–Dec   J F M A M J J A S O N D

Long-billed Pipit

Differs from similar African Pipit by having buff, not white outer-tail feathers, more uniform markings on the face and much less defined streaking on the breast. The bill is not unusually long but does have a pinkish, not yellowish base. Juv. is more heavily streaked on breast and back. **Habitat**: Rocky grassland. **Status**: Locally common. **Voice**: High-pitched, 2–3-note song, 'tchreep-tritit-churup', usually from prominent perch; sharp 'wheet' call. (Nicholsonkoester)

18 cm | **Br**: Aug–Apr   J F M A M J J A S O N D

African Pipit

The pipit most likely to be seen in the open veld or grassland near towns and cities. It is fairly nondescript: buff and brown with streaking on the breast, and prominent white outer-tail feathers visible in flight. Always feeds on the ground, where it runs short distances, stops to pick up food and then stands with a very upright posture. **Habitat**: Open grassland and fields. **Status**: Common. **Voice**: Song is a repeated 'trrit trrit trrit' given in display flight. (Gewone koester)

16–17 cm | Br: Aug–May   J F M A M J J A S O N D

Yellow-throated Longclaw

A long-legged and long-toed grassland bird that has a proportionally short, white-tipped tail that is conspicuous in flight. The underparts are bright canary-yellow and there is a broad black gorget. When flushed, the bird flies with jerky wing beats and glides with its tail spread, showing the white tips. **Habitat**: Grassland, often near wetlands and well-grassed savanna woodland. **Status**: Common. **Voice**: Loud, whistled 'phooooeeect' or series of loud whistles, frequently uttered from top of small trees; also calls in flight. (Geelkeelkalkoentjie)

20–22 cm | Br: Jul–Mar   J F M A M J J A S O N D

Cape Longclaw   E

Most often encountered when flushed in the veld: in flight the tail is usually held spread, showing the white tips, and the flight is on stiffly held wings that are kept spread below body level. The back is well streaked and mottled. Only on landing, and when the bird is facing the viewer, can the brilliant orange throat, surrounded by a black band and duller orange-yellow underparts, be seen. **Habitat**: Wide range of coastal and upland grassland. **Status**: Common. **Voice**: Fairly melodious song, 'cheewit-cheewit', often in flight; nasal 'wheea' alarm call. (Oranjekeelkalkoentjie)

20 cm | Br: Jul–Apr   J F M A M J J A S O N D

Crimson-breasted Shrike NE

Unmistakable: one of the most startlingly-coloured birds of the dry bushveld. The brilliant crimson underparts contrast with the jet-black upperparts, which are offset by a white flash down the wing. Although very brightly coloured, it can be difficult to see as it tends to skulk in the undergrowth. However, it often feeds on the ground and sometimes in fairly open areas. **Habitat**: Acacia thickets in arid savanna, dry river courses and semi-arid scrub. **Status**: Common. **Voice**: Harsh 'trrrrr'; whistled 'qwip-qwip' duet. (Rooiborslaksman)

23 cm | Br: May, Aug–Feb   J F M A M J J A S O N D

Magpie Shrike

Unmistakable. The very long, black, wispy tail and all-black plumage dotted with white on the wings are diagnostic. Female has shorter tail with more white on the flanks. Juv. is shorter tailed than both ads and is a dull dark brown, finely barred with black. When feeding, sits atop exposed perch and then drops to the ground to retrieve its prey. **Habitat**: Acacia savanna. **Status**: Common; often in small groups of 4–8 birds. **Voice**: Liquid, whistled 'peeleeo'. (Langstertlaksman)

40–50 cm | Br: Aug–Mar | J F M A M J J A S O N D

Red-backed Shrike

A small, colourful shrike with a grey head and rump, black mask through the eye, a black tail and very conspicuous chestnut back and wings. Female is drab brown above with a pale eye-stripe and fine brown barring on the underparts. A typical shrike, it perches in exposed positions from where it can scan the ground for the insects on which it feeds. **Habitat**: Savanna, broad-leaved woodland and thornveld. **Status**: Common Palaearctic migrant. **Voice**: Harsh 'chak, chak'; soft, warbler-like song. (Rooiruglaksman)

juv.

16–18 cm | Br: n/a | J F M A M J J A S O N D

Lesser Grey Shrike

Much larger than Red-backed Shrike and has a more extensive black mask that encompasses the forehead, has a grey, not chestnut back and predominantly black, not brownish wings. Also shows a white primary base on the folded wing and has clear white, not peach-tinged underparts. Juv. is larger than juv. and female Red-backed Shrike and has buffier, less barred underparts. **Habitat**: Arid savanna and semi-desert scrub. **Status**: Common Palaearctic migrant Oct–Apr. **Voice**: Soft 'chuk'; warbled song, heard before return migration. (Gryslaksman)

20–22 cm | Br: n/a | J F M A M J J A S O N D

Common Fiscal

Resembles Fiscal Flycatcher but is more robust in build, has a much longer tail and has white shoulder patches. It also has a more powerful bill, which is obviously hooked. Female has a rufous patch on the flanks. Imm. is mottled brown above and has grey barring below. A common and familiar bird, which hunts from perches in exposed situations. **Habitat**: Widespread throughout region, except dense forest. **Status**: Common. **Voice**: Harsh, grating call; song is melodious and jumbled, often with harsher notes and mimicry of other birds' calls. (Fiskaallaksman)

21–23 cm | Br: Jan–Dec | J F M A M J J A S O N D

Southern Boubou E

Replaces Tropical Boubou in the S and their ranges hardly overlap. Differs chiefly by having rufous flanks and belly. Vaguely resembles Common Fiscal, but tail is much shorter and this species skulks in thicket and is difficult to observe; rarely sits on exposed perches. **Habitat**: Forest edge, thickets and dense coastal scrub. **Status**: Common. **Voice**: Variable duet with basic notes of 'boo-boo' followed by whistled 'whee-ooo'; also harsh, scolding calls. (Suidelike waterfiskaal)

20–22 cm | Br: May, Aug–Mar | J F M A M J J A S O N D

Tropical Boubou

Replaces Southern Boubou in the N and is easily told apart by having much whiter underparts, slightly tinged with pinkish-peach. Easily confused with Southern Boubou, but paler below showing a marked contrast between its black upperparts and pinkish underparts. Juv. is duller than ad. and spotted with buff above and below. **Habitat**: Thickets, riverine and evergreen forests, and gardens. **Status**: Common. **Voice**: Loud, ringing duet, typically 'wee hooo' or 'wee hooo hooo'; also various whistles and harsh, croaking calls. (Tropiese waterfiskaal)

19–22 cm | Br: Jan–Dec | J F M A M J J A S O N D

Black-crowned Tchagra

This species is shy and furtive and when flushed from cover will fly quickly to the next bush, briefly showing its chestnut wings and white-tipped, black tail. Only when the diagnostic black line down the centre of the crown is seen can a positive identification be made. Sometimes feeds on ground but mostly is seen as it moves through the lower tangles of bush. **Habitat**: Savanna, thickets and riverine scrub. **Status**: Fairly common. **Voice**: Song is characteristic, slightly mournful, loud, whistled 'whee-cheree, cherooo, cheree-cherooo'. (Swartkroontjagra)

19–22 cm | Br: Aug–Apr | J F M A M J J A S O N D

Brown-crowned Tchagra

Most likely to be confused with larger Southern Tchagra, but it is unlikely they would be seen together as their ranges and habitats do not overlap. However, the main differences are that this species has a much paler crown and forehead and its broad white eyebrow stripe is narrowly bordered with black. It is also paler on the underparts. **Habitat**: Thick tangles and undergrowth in savanna and woodland. **Status**: Common. **Voice**: Aerial display flight and song are very similar to those of Southern Tchagra. (Rooivlerktjagra)

17–19 cm | Br: Sep–Mar | J F M A M J J A S O N D

Southern Tchagra   E

Larger than similar Brown-crowned Tchagra with a much stronger and more robust bill. Also has a darker crown lacking a black edge and has darker and greyer underparts. Confusion should not arise with Brown-crowned Tchagra because it is very unlikely they would ever occur together. Forages on the ground, scraping leaf litter with its bill and feet to expose prey items. **Habitat**: Coastal scrub, forest edges and thickets. **Status**: Common. **Voice**: Song, given in aerial display, is 'wee-chee-chee-cheee', descending in pitch. (Grysborstjagra)

17–21 cm | Br: Mar, Aug–Dec | J F M A M J J A S O N D

Grey-headed Bushshrike

A much larger version of the Orange-breasted Bush-Shrike with a more massive, hooked bill, a pale, not dark eye and lacking yellow forehead and eye-stripe. Shows a white area at base of bill towards eye. Juv. has variable amounts of orange on breast, from just a slight wash to deep orange. **Habitat**: Thickets in acacia savanna and broad-leaved woodland. **Status**: Common. **Voice**: Drawn-out 'oooooop' (hence colloquial name 'Ghostbird'); 'tic-tic-oooop'. (Spookvoël)

24–26 cm | Br: Apr, Jul–Feb | J F M A M J J A S O N D

Bokmakierie   E

This robust shrike is a familiar bird in many areas and its call is commonly heard. The ad. is easily recognised by its grey head, green back and bright yellow underparts with a black gorget. Imm. lacks the black gorget, but the undertail, like that of the ad., has conspicuous yellow tips that are obvious in flight. Display consists of head bowing and tail raising by both ads. as they face each other. **Habitat**: Shrublands, Karoo scrub, grassland with scattered bushes and suburban gardens. **Status**: Common. **Voice**: Very varied whistles, but usually duetted 'bok-bok-kik'. (Bokmakierie)

22–23 cm | Br: Jan–Dec | J F M A M J J A S O N D

Orange-breasted Bushshrike

Most similar to Grey-headed Bush-shrike but very much smaller and with a less robust bill. It further differs by having an orangey-yellow, not grey-and-white forehead and eyebrow stripe and a dark, not yellow eye. Juv. is duller than ad. and lacks the yellow on the head. **Habitat**: Acacia savanna and riverine forests. **Status**: Common. **Voice**: Song is frequently repeated 'poo-poo-poo-pooooo', fading towards end; deeper 'pu pu pu pu'; harsher 'titit-eeezz'. (Oranjeborsboslaksman)

16–18 cm | Br: Aug–Mar | J F M A M J J A S O N D

White-crested Helmetshrike

Always seen in small groups flitting through open woodland in follow-my-leader style. Flocks are conspicuous when they take flight as they show their pied black-and-white plumage with a lot of white in the wings and tail. At rest the bird shows a grey crest, white collar, clear white underparts and a black tail. **Habitat**: Mixed woodland and acacia savanna. **Status**: Common resident, with local movements and occasional invasions beyond its normal range. **Voice**: Repeated 'cherow', often taken up by group in chorus. (Withelmlaksman)

17–20 cm | Br: Apr, Aug–Feb | J F M A M J J A S O N D

Southern White-crowned Shrike   NE

A fairly large and robust shrike and the only one to have a white crown and forehead. The black mask and black expansion on ear coverts to nape rule out confusion with Southern Pied and Bare-cheeked babblers. Juv. is paler than ad. with a mottled greyish crown. **Habitat**: Mixed dry woodland and acacia savanna. **Status**: Common; usually in groups of 3–6 birds. **Voice**: Shrill, whistling 'kree, kree, kree'; bleating and harsh chattering (Kremetartlaksman)

24 cm | Br: Sep–May | J F M A M J J A S O N D

Brubru

Might be mistaken for a batis but is much larger, has a thicker, hooked bill and a broad, straight eyebrow stripe. The combination of a chequered back, broad white eyebrow stripe and chestnut flank stripe all should point to its identification. Female is duller than male. **Habitat**: Dry acacia savanna and open broad-leaved woodland. **Status**: Common. **Voice**: Soft, trilling 'prrrrr' given by male, often answered 'eeeu' by female. (Bontroklaksman)

12–13.5 cm | Br: Jan–Dec | J F M A M J J A S O N D

Black-backed Puffback

This small shrike is a noisy and conspicuous member of bird parties foraging in the mid- and top canopy. Male has a jet-black cap and obvious red eye, a grey-and-black back and a diagnostic white rump. In display, male fluffs his rump feathers into a fur-like white ball and dashes through the foliage in pursuit of female. Female is paler than male. **Habitat**: Woodland, thickets and forest canopy. **Status**: Common. **Voice**: Sharp, repeated 'chick, weeo'; in flight, male utters loud 'chok chok chok'. (Sneeubal)

16–18 cm | Br: Jan–Dec | J F M A M J J A S O N D

Greater Blue-eared Starling

Differs from similar Cape Glossy Starling by its dark blue, not green ears and distinctive blue, not green belly and flanks. It also has a much sturdier bill and more pronounced black spots on the wing coverts. Juv. is a very much duller version of ad. and has a dark eye and blackish underparts. **Habitat**: Savanna and mopane woodland. **Status**: Common. **Voice**: Distinctive, nasal 'squee-aar' (unlike any call of Cape Glossy Starling); warbled song. (Groot-blouoorglansspreeu)

23–24 cm | Br: Aug–Jan | J F M A M J J A S O N D

Cape Glossy Starling

The iridescent coloration of this bird is evident only in direct sunlight; at a distance, it can appear black. The bright orange eye is wide, staring and button-like. There are two rows of black spots on the wing coverts and the bird can be distinguished from the Black-bellied Starling by its brighter glossy plumage and by having an iridescent greenish-blue, not black belly. It occurs in pairs or small parties and does not normally form large flocks. **Habitat**: Savanna, mixed woodland and gardens. **Status**: Common. **Voice**: Song is slurred 'trrr-chree-chrrrr'. (Kleinglansspreeu)

25 cm | Br: Sep–Feb | J F M A M J J A S O N D

Violet-backed Starling

Male of this small starling is an unusual glossy amethyst colour on the head, throat and upperparts but, at a distance, it appears black and white. Female is very different: her drab brown upperparts and heavily streaked underparts impart a thrush-like appearance. This species is seen in pairs or small groups in trees, rarely on the ground. **Habitat**: Most woodland, but avoids dense forest. **Status**: Common resident and intra-African migrant. **Voice**: Soft but sharp 'tip, tip'; song is short series of buzzy whistles. (Witborsspreeu)

15–17 cm | Br: Oct–Jan | J F M A M J J A S O N D

Black-bellied Starling

Resembles the Cape Glossy Starling but is less glossy, with a matt black belly and flanks, and has a yellow, not orange eye. It is also noticeably smaller and more slender than the Cape Glossy Starling and has a proportionately longer tail. It frequently forms large flocks out of the br. season and is much noisier and more demonstrative than the Cape Glossy Starling. **Habitat**: Coastal and riverine forests. **Status**: Locally common; irregular visitor in extreme S of range. **Voice**: Harsh, chippering notes interspersed with shrill whistles. (Swartpensglansspreeu)

18–21 cm | Br: Oct–Jan | J F M A M J J A S O N D

Burchell's Starling NE

Could be confused with Meve's Starling but altogether much more bulky, with a broader, not narrow wedge-shaped tail. It is also a glossier green, not blue-green. Differs from all other glossy starlings by being larger and having a much longer tail and dark, not orange or yellow eyes. Juv. is a duller version of ad. **Habitat**: Savanna and dry, broad-leaved woodland. **Status**: Common. **Voice**: Song is jumble of throaty chortles and chuckles. (Grootglansspreeu)

32–34 cm | **Br: Sep–Mar** | J F M A M J J A S O N D

Meve's Starling

The long, narrow, pointed tail is diagnostic on this glossy starling. Differs from Burchell's Starling by its smaller, more compact body and longer tail. This species and Burchell's Starling are the only glossy starlings to have dark eyes (in ad.). **Habitat**: Tall mopane woodland and riverine forest. Favours well-wooded areas, especially stands of baobab trees and their surrounding thickets. **Status**: Locally common. **Voice**: Harsh 'keeeaaaa' and churring notes. (Langstertglansspreeu)

34–36 cm | **Br: Nov–Apr** | J F M A M J J A S O N D

Pale-winged Starling NE

At rest, very similar to male Red-winged Starling but differs by having a bright orange, not dark eye. The creamy white wing patches identify this bird and are diagnostic but are not usually visible until the bird is in flight. Unlike Red-winged Starling, female is similar to male. Juv. is less glossy than ad. and has a dark eye. **Habitat**: Rocky ravines and cliffs in semi-arid and arid regions. **Status**: Common resident and local nomad; sometimes forms mixed flocks with Red-winged Starling. **Voice**: Ringing 'preeoo' in flight. (Bleekvlerkspreeu)

26–28 cm | **Br: Sep–Apr** | J F M A M J J A S O N D

Red-winged Starling

This large, long-tailed starling is easily recognised in flight when the bright chestnut primaries can clearly be seen; at rest, the chestnut is not normally visible on the folded wing. Male is a slightly glossy dark blue, while female is duller, with a dark grey head and breast, but she still shows the chestnut primaries. Sometimes occurs in large flocks. **Habitat**: Rocky ravines, cliffs and gardens. Disperses widely when not breeding. **Status**: Common. **Voice**: Clear, whistled 'cherleeeeoo'; variety of musical whistles and harsh, grating alarm call. (Rooivlerkspreeu)

27–30 cm | **Br: Sep–Apr** | J F M A M J J A S O N D

Common Myna

A starling-sized bird which, in flight, shows conspicuous white patches in the wings and a white-tipped tail. At rest it appears brown with a glossy black head, a bright yellow bill, bare yellow skin around the eyes, and yellow legs. A noisy inhabitant of cities and towns where it feeds on open lawns and fields and along roadsides. **Habitat**: Urban and suburban regions. **Status**: Locally common. Gathers in large roosts in the evenings and is generally considered a pest. **Voice**: Jumbled titters and chattering. (Indiese spreeu)

25 cm | **Br:** Jan–Dec   J F M A M J J A S O N D

Common Starling

During the br. season the ad. is an iridescent green, blue and black but appears all-black when not seen in sunlight; the bill is bright yellow. The non-br. bird is conspicuously spotted with white and has a dark bill, while imm. is brown and has a paler throat. Sometimes occurs in large flocks, especially when roosting or feeding in fields. **Habitat**: Wide range, from cities to open farmland, but always close to human habitation. **Status**: Common in S Africa. **Voice**: Song includes mimicry, whistles and chattering. (Europese spreeu)

20–22 cm | **Br:** Sep–Dec   J F M A M J J A S O N D

non-br.

Wattled Starling

In flight appears similar to imm. Common Starling but the Wattled Starling has a pale rump. A greyish bird with black wings and tail, during the br. season the male attains wattles and becomes very conspicuous, showing his black-and-yellow patterned head. When breeding, this species forms large colonies that nest in trees and bushes. **Habitat**: Grassland, savanna and open woodland. Often perches on livestock. **Status**: Common resident and nomad; breeds colonially; regularly joins flocks of other starlings. **Voice**: Various hisses and cackles; 'sreeeeo' note. (Lelspreeu)

19–21 cm | **Br:** Sep–Mar   J F M A M J J A S O N D

Pied Starling   E

This large, dark brown, almost black starling is readily identified by its conspicuous white vent and undertail coverts. At closer range the pale eye and the yellow base to the bill are noticeable. Feeds on the ground, often among livestock, and will search for ectoparasites on animals' backs. Forms large flocks in early morning and evening. **Habitat**: Grassland and Karoo scrub, often around farmyards and stock. **Status**: Common; usually in flocks. Breeds colonially in holes in river or sand banks. **Voice**: Loud 'skeer-kerrra-kerrra'; warbling song. (Witgatspreeu)

27–28 cm | **Br:** Jan–Dec   J F M A M J J A S O N D

Red-billed Oxpecker

This species is usually seen peering over the back of a large mammal and giving its scolding call notes. As it scrambles over the animal's body looking for ticks, the large red bill and the bare yellow skin around the eye are clearly visible. Young birds have a dark bill with a yellow base. When not feeding, small groups sit in trees or fly between herds with their starling-like flight. **Habitat**: Savanna; in association with game and cattle. **Status**: Locally common; usually in flocks. **Voice**: Scolding 'churrrr'; hissing 'zzzzzzist'. (Rooibekrenostervoël)

19–21 cm | Br: Sep–Mar | J F M A M J J A S O N D

Gurney's Sugarbird   E

Not likely to be confused with the Cape Sugarbird because their ranges do not overlap. Differs from the Cape Sugarbird by being smaller, shorter tailed and has a conspicuous russet crown and broad russet breast band. Does not have the demonstrative bounding display flight of the Cape Sugarbird. **Habitat**: Stands of flowering proteas and aloes in mountainous regions. **Status**: Common, localised resident; some move to lower altitudes in winter. **Voice**: Rattling song, higher pitched and more melodious than Cape Sugarbird's. (Rooiborssuikervoël)

♂ 29 cm
♀ 23 cm | Br: Apr, Jun, Sep–Feb | J F M A M J J A S O N D

Cape Sugarbird   E

Male is easily identified by its combination of an extremely long and wispy tail, long decurved bill, greyish-brown upperparts and speckled drab underparts with a bright lemon vent and undertail coverts. Female and imm. are similar to male but have shorter tails. In courtship and display the male dances in mid-air with wings flapping vigorously and his long tail partially spread as he repeatedly flicks it over his back. **Habitat**: Fynbos; visits gardens and coastal scrub after breeding. **Status**: Common. **Voice**: Rattling song. (Kaapse suikervoël)

♂ 34–44 cm
♀ 25–29 cm | Br: Mar–Nov | J F M A M J J A S O N D

Malachite Sunbird

Largest sunbird in the region and the only one with an all-metallic green plumage with long tail projections. Male in 'eclipse' plumage loses his green sheen for a short period and then resembles female. Female is olive-brown above and has yellowish underparts but is distinguished by her large size and long, decurved bill. **Habitat**: Fynbos, grassland and mountain scrub; sea-level in S to 3 500 m in N. **Status**: Common resident and local migrant. **Voice**: Piercing 'tseep-tseep'; song series of twittering notes. Male's call is a high-pitched ringing 'zing-zing'. (Jangroentjie)

♂ 25 cm
♀ 15 cm | Br: Jan–Dec | J F M A M J J A S O N D

♀

Orange-breasted Sunbird E

The only small sunbird in the region to have pointed tail projections. The head is an iridescent green and blue, the back a dull olive, and the breast and belly bright orange. In the fynbos habitat, female could be confused only with female Southern Double-collared Sunbird but is noticeably larger and is a more uniform olive-green above and below. **Habitat**: Fynbos and adjacent gardens. **Status**: Common. **Voice**: Call metallic, nasal twang; rapid 'ticks' given in pursuit flight; song subdued jumble of notes; mimics other species. (Oranjeborssuikerbekkie)

♂ 15 cm
♀ 12 cm | Br: Jan–Dec   J F M A M J J A S O N D

Scarlet-chested Sunbird

A large, chunky sunbird, the male is unmistakable: it has a matt black body and bright scarlet breast. At close range the iridescent blue flecks on the scarlet breast can be seen. Female resembles female Amethyst Sunbird but has more mottled underparts and lacks the buff moustachial stripes of that species. Male is bold and conspicuous, chasing other birds from his territory. **Habitat**: Woodland, savanna and suburban gardens. **Status**: Common. **Voice**: Loud, whistled 'cheeup, chup, toop, toop, toop' song. (Rooiborssuikerbekkie)

15 cm | Br: Jan–Dec   J F M A M J J A S O N D

Amethyst Sunbird

Although the same length as the Scarlet-chested Sunbird, it is more slender and has a neater, more compact body shape. Male is easily distinguished by his matt black plumage that is relieved only by an iridescent greenish-violet patch on the throat and shoulder, and a bronze-green forehead. Female closely resembles female Scarlet-chested Sunbird but has obvious buff moustachial stripes and is paler and less streaked below. **Habitat**: Woodland, forest edge and gardens. **Status**: Common. **Voice**: Quite deep, fast, twittering song; loud, harsh calls. (Swartsuikerbekkie)

15 cm | Br: Jan–Dec   J F M A M J J A S O N D

Olive Sunbird

A drab olive, greenish-brown sunbird with paler underparts. Both sexes have yellow pectoral tufts but they are not usually visible except when alarmed or in display. Confusion likely with female Greater or Southern double-collared sunbirds but they are overall greyer and paler. **Habitat**: Coastal, riverine and montane forests. **Status**: Common; usually the most abundant forest sunbird in its range. **Voice**: Call sharp 'tuk, tuk, tuk'; song series of descending, piping notes, accelerating in pace, and sometimes increasing in pitch at end. (Olyfsuikerbekkie)

11–15 cm | Br: Sep–Mar   J F M A M J J A S O N D

Collared Sunbird

This tiny sunbird is unmistakable. The combination of bright yellow underparts and metallic green head and back plus a short bill all help identify this species. Female lacks the green throat and breast and has uniform yellow underparts. Very warbler-like in habits. A common member of bird parties, especially with flocks of white-eyes and other small passerines. **Habitat**: Forest, dense woodland and gardens. **Status**: Common. **Voice**: Soft 'tswee'; a harsh, chirpy song. (Kortbeksuikerbekkie)

10 cm | **Br:** Jun–Mar | J F M A M J J A S O N D

♀

White-bellied Sunbird

A very small sunbird and the only one in the region to have a bottle-green head and back, and a white belly. Female is nondescript and looks like a small grey warbler with a white belly, but the long, decurved bill confirms that it is a sunbird. Male is conspicuous during the br. season when he perches high to deliver his fast, buzzy song. **Habitat**: Dry woodland, savanna and gardens. **Status**: Common. **Voice**: Loud 'pichee, pichee', followed by rapid tinkle of notes. (Witpenssuikerbekkie)

11 cm | **Br:** Jun–Apr | J F M A M J J A S O N D

♀

Dusky Sunbird   NE

Appears black and white but has a slight metallic sheen to the breast, head and back and this combined with the contrasting white belly and vent is diagnostic in the male. Pectoral tufts are orange. Male's plumage is very variable but usually shows remnants of the black body plumage. Female resembles female Southern Double-collared Sunbird but is paler and greyer. **Habitat**: Arid savanna, acacia thickets and Karoo scrub. **Status**: Common; wanders into more mesic areas in some years. **Voice**: 'Chrrrr-chrrrr'; short, warbling song. (Namakwasuikerbekkie)

10 cm | **Br:** Jan–Dec | J F M A M J J A S O N D

Greater Double-collared Sunbird   E

Within its range it is likely to be confused only with the Southern Double-collared Sunbird, from which it can be distinguished as it is considerably larger, has a longer, thicker bill and a broader scarlet breast band. Females of both species are olive and dark brown but female Greater Double-collared is noticeably greener on the underparts and has a longer, heavier bill. Very active and restless. **Habitat**: Occurs in mountainous terrain. **Status**: Common. **Voice**: A harsh 'tchut-tchut-tchut' and a fast, warbling song. (Groot-rooibandsuikerbekkie)

14 cm | **Br:** Jan–Dec | J F M A M J J A S O N D

♀ ♂

Southern Double-collared Sunbird   E

Confusion arises with the Greater Double-collared Sunbird, from which it can be distinguished by its smaller size, shorter and finer decurved bill, and a much narrower scarlet breast band. Female differs from female Greater Double-collared Sunbird by the smaller bill character and from female Orange-breasted Sunbird by being greyer on the underparts. **Habitat**: Found in coastal scrub, fynbos and forest edge. **Status**: Common. **Voice**: The call is a harsh 'chee-chee'. (Kleinrooibandsuikerbekkie)

12 cm | Br: Jan–Dec   J F M A M J J A S O N D

Marico Sunbird

The male has an iridescent purple band that contrasts with the black belly. Head and back are a metallic, iridescent greenish-blue and the bill is long and decurved. Female is a drab olive-brown above with paler, streaked underparts and poses complex identification problems with many other similar female sunbirds; however, her long, robust and decurved bill is the distinguishing feature. **Habitat**: Frequents thornveld and dry, broad-leaved woodland. **Status**: Common. **Voice**: Long series of rapid 'tsip tsip tsip'; fast warbling song. (Maricosuikerbekkie)

11–13.5 cm | Br: Aug–Feb   J F M A M J J A S O N D

House Sparrow

Male has a grey crown and rump, black bib, pale cheeks, chestnut mantle and a white wing bar. Female is a drab greyish-brown with a streaked mantle, a buffish eyebrow stripe and paler off-white underparts. A displaying male will droop his wings, cock his tail and hold his head back as he hops around a female. **Habitat**: Towns, cities and gardens; usually close to human habitation. **Status**: Introduced; locally common; sometimes forms flocks of up to 50 birds which may occur away from built-up areas. **Voice**: Various chirps, chips and 'chissick'. (Huismossie)

14 cm | Br: Jan–Dec   J F M A M J J A S O N D

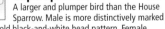

Cape Sparrow   NE

A larger and plumper bird than the House Sparrow. Male is more distinctively marked with a bold black-and-white head pattern. Female has a chestnut mantle and a shadow impression of male's head pattern. Occurs mostly in small groups or pairs but at times forms large flocks and joins parties of bishops, weavers and queleas feeding on old grain fields and crops. **Habitat**: Grassland, fields and large gardens; common in urban areas in some parts of range, but not in others. **Status**: Common. **Voice**: Series of musical cheeps. (Gewone mossie)

15 cm | Br: Jan–Dec   J F M A M J J A S O N D

Yellow-throated Petronia

Mistaken for White-browed Sparrow-Weaver because of broad buffy eyebrow stripe just above the eye and can appear very white in some lights and plumages. However, the Yellow-throated Petronia is very much smaller, lacks a white rump and has buff underparts. This species can also resemble a female House Sparrow, but its eyebrow stripe is broader, it has two buff wing bars and would seldom be found in the same habitat. **Habitat**: Lightly wooded areas, dry grassland. **Status**: Locally common resident and nomad. **Voice**: Sparrow-like chirps. (Geelvlekmossie)

15 cm | Br. Aug–Mar | J F M A M J J A S O N D

Southern Grey-headed Sparrow

Might be mistaken for female House Sparrow but the very obvious grey head should eliminate confusion. Occurs in the vicinity of farm buildings and yards where it associates with Cape and House sparrows; more often seen in open woodland, particularly on dead trees in which it can nest. **Habitat**: Prefers mixed woodland; occurs in gardens in some areas but generally avoids urban areas. **Status**: Common. **Voice**: Various chirping notes, 'tchep tchierp tchep'; brief alarm rattle. (Gryskopmossie)

15 cm | Br: Jan–Apr, Jul–Sep | J F M A M J J A S O N D

Red-billed Buffalo Weaver

The only large, black, sparrow-like bird in the region. It has a robust red bill and in flight shows white patches in the primary feathers. Female and imm. are browner versions of male. Feeds mostly on the ground; when disturbed, groups will fly up into trees. Their nests are large, untidy bundles of thorny sticks, placed in trees and windmills. **Habitat**: Dry woodland and savanna. Breeds communally in large trees or on electricity pylons. **Status**: Common resident and local migrant. **Voice**: Song is 'chip-chip-doodley-doodley-dooo'; also harsh calls. (Buffelwewer)

21–24 cm | Br: Sep–Jun | J F M A M J J A S O N D

non-br.

White-browed Sparrow-Weaver

This large and chunky, short-tailed weaver is unmistakable. The broad white eyebrow stripe that extends onto the nape, combined with the white double wing bar and conspicuous white rump are all diagnostic. Birds in the N have speckled breasts. Males have all-black bills and female's is a paler pinkish colour. **Habitat**: Acacia savanna and dry woodland. **Status**: Common; in small groups. **Voice**: Harsh 'chik-chik'; loud, liquid 'cheeoop-preeoo-chop' whistle. (Koringvoël)

17–19 cm | Br: Jan–Dec | J F M A M J J A S O N D

Thick-billed Weaver

This large weaver is the only one with such a massive, thick bill, and dark brown plumage relieved only by white patches in the wings and a white forehead. Female is markedly different, being brown above and paler and heavily streaked below, but still shows the large bill. Small flocks are often seen as they fly to and from their roosts, giving their 'tweek-tweek' call. In flight, males' white wing patches appear translucent. **Habitat**: Occurs in evergreen and coastal forests, and in reed beds. **Status**: Locally common. **Voice**: Harsh chattering. (Dikbekwewer)

15–17 cm | Br: Oct–Mar | J F M A M J J A S O N D

Sociable Weaver   E

The pale grey bill, black chin, black buff-edged flank feathers and scaly-patterned back render this bird easy to identify. Very gregarious; sometimes builds enormous nests that appear to thatch the trees and telephone poles in which they are built. Juv. lacks the black face of the ad. and has very much reduced flank markings. **Habitat**: Semi-arid savanna and Karoo scrub. **Status**: Common. **Voice**: Chattering 'chicker-chicker' call. (Versamelvoël)

14 cm | Br: Jan–Dec | J F M A M J J A S O N D

Village Weaver

Male in br. plumage is the only black-faced weaver to have a yellow-and-black speckled back. When not br. male loses his bright yellow plumage and attains the drab greenish and olive colour of female and imm. It is then exceedingly difficult to differentiate from other weavers in similar plumage. **Habitat**: Savanna, fields and gardens. Breeds colonially in trees, palms and reed beds; nest is rather untidy, with a short entrance tube. **Status**: Common; often in large flocks. **Voice**: Throaty 'chuck-chuck'; buzzy, swizzling notes. (Bontrugwewer)

14–16 cm | Br: Aug–Apr | J F M A M J J A S O N D

Southern Masked Weaver

The br. male can be distinguished from male Village Weaver by its uniform yellowish-green back and by the greater extent of black on the head, especially on the forehead. The non-br. male, female and imm. are alike, having yellowish underparts and olive-brown upperparts. **Habitat**: Savanna, grassland, fields and gardens. Breeds singly or in small colonies in trees or reeds; nest is neat ball with a short entrance tube. **Status**: Common and widespread. **Voice**: Sharp 'zik, zik'; usual swizzling weaver notes. (Swartkeelgeelvink)

11–14.5 cm | Br: Jul–Apr | J F M A M J J A S O N D

Lesser Masked Weaver

Slightly smaller and more compact than the similar Southern Masked-Weaver, this species is easily distinguished in br. plumage by having more extensive black on the head, encompassing the crown and extending onto the throat in a rounded, not pointed bib. Further differs from the Southern Masked-Weaver in all plumages by having a pale, not red eye. Out of br. season it forms mixed flocks with other weavers. **Habitat**: Savanna and woodland. Breeds colonially in trees and reeds near water. **Status**: Locally common. **Voice**: Typical swizzling song. (Kleingeelvink)

13–14 cm | Br: Apr–Mar   J F M A M J J A S O N D

Spectacled Weaver

A very bright yellow, unmasked weaver. Both sexes show a dark line through the eye, have sharp pointed bills, pale yellow eyes and an orangey wash across the head. Male has a small black chin. Juv. resembles female but has a dark eye and the black eye-stripe only develops in its first year. Woven nest has the longest funnel of all weavers' nests. **Habitat**: Forest edge, moist woodland, thickets and gardens. Breeds singly. **Status**: Common; usually in pairs. **Voice**: Distinctive, descending 'dee-dee-dee-dee-dee'; harsh trills and swizzling song. (Brilwewer)

14–15 cm | Br: Sep–Mar   J F M A M J J A S O N D

Red-headed Weaver

Male unmistakable with its bright scarlet-red head, back and breast. Female is duller and has yellow replacing the red of male's head, back and breast and has a pale pinkish bill. Juv. similar to female but is duller and has a dark bill. The untidy woven nest is often hung on telephone wires. **Habitat**: Woodland, savanna and gardens. **Status**: Locally common. **Voice**: Squeaky 'cherra cherra'; harsher calls and swizzling. (Rooikopwewer)

13–14 cm | Br: Jul–Feb   J F M A M J J A S O N D

Cape Weaver   E

Most likely to be confused with the Yellow Weaver, but differs by being larger, less brilliant yellow in colour, having an orange- or rust-coloured wash over the face, and by having a cream, not red eye. The non-br. male resembles the olive and yellowish female and imm. Male will hang from a completed nest and sway from side to side, flapping his wings and giving the swizzling notes typical of weavers. **Habitat**: Grassland and scrub. Colonial breeder in reeds and trees. **Status**: Common. **Voice**: Harsh, hysterical swizzling song; 'chack' contact call. (Kaapse wewer)

17 cm | Br: Jun–Feb   J F M A M J J A S O N D

Yellow Weaver

Male in br. plumage is best distinguished from br. male Cape Weaver by its smaller size, more vivid golden-yellow plumage, less extensive wash of orange on the face and a bright red, not cream eye. The non-br. male, female and imm. are similar in appearance; unlike other weavers in alternate plumage, they have a distinct pale yellow throat and breast that is sharply demarcated from the white underparts. **Habitat**: Woodland, savanna and gardens. Breeds colonially in reed beds and trees near water. **Status**: Locally common; in flocks. **Voice**: Soft 'chucks' and swizzling. (Geelwewer)

11–14 cm | **Br**: Sep–Feb   J F M A M J J A S O N D

Red-billed Quelea

Male in br. plumage is unmistakable with his black face bordered with red and his bright red bill and legs. The non-br. male and female are very sparrow-like but still show the red bill and legs. The br. female has a horn-coloured bill. This species is best known for concentrating in hundreds of thousands of birds that fly in tightly packed flocks. **Habitat**: Savanna and fields, where it is a significant pest. **Status**: Common nomad; at times abundant, in flocks numbering millions. **Voice**: Song is jumble of harsh and melodious notes; flocks make chittering noise. (Rooibekkwelea)

11–13 cm | **Br**: Nov–Apr   J F M A M J J A S O N D

Southern Red Bishop

Identified by the combination of its bright orange and black plumage. Female, imm. and non-br. male are not easily distinguished from the similarly plumaged Yellow-crowned Bishop but this species appears darker and has more heavily streaked underparts. Male performs a display flight in which he fluffs out his feathers and, with rapid wing beats, whizzes to and fro. **Habitat**: Grassland, savanna and fields, usually associated with water. **Status**: Common; highly gregarious. **Voice**: Buzzing, chirping song; 'cheet-cheet' flight call. (Rooivink)

10–11 cm | **Br**: Jan–Dec   J F M A M J J A S O N D

Yellow-crowned Bishop

Most often seen with widows and weavers in very large, mixed flocks when all the birds appear as unidentifiable 'little brown jobs' with mottled and streaked brown and buff plumages. This species most closely resembles the Southern Red Bishop in this obscure plumage but is noticeably smaller, more compact and is paler overall with reduced streaking on the breast and flanks. Male in br. plumage is easily identified by his yellow-and-black coloration. **Habitat**: Flooded grassland, vleis and marshes. **Status**: Locally common. **Voice**: Buzzing and chirping notes. (Goudgeelvink)

9.5–10.5 cm | **Br**: Oct–Apr   J F M A M J J A S O N D

Yellow Bishop

All show some diagnostic yellow or red markings. This species has a bright yellow rump and lower back and a yellow shoulder patch. Female shows a dull yellow rump, which distinguishes her from all other female widowbirds. Male in non-br. plumage resembles female but, in flight, shows a yellow rump and shoulder patch. **Habitat:** Frequents damp, grassy areas, bracken-covered mountain valleys and fynbos. **Status:** Common. **Voice:** Displaying males give high-pitched 'zeet, zeet, zeet' or harsh 'zzzzzzzzt'. (Kaapse flap)

15 cm | **Br:** Jul–Apr   J F M A M J J A S O N D

Red-collared Widowbird

Resembles a diminutive Long-tailed Widowbird and at a distance they might be confused, but this species lacks the red shoulder. At closer range the red crescentic marking on the throat can easily be seen. The non-br. male, female and imm. are very similar to the plainly-coloured bishops and other widowbirds, but this species shows a boldly striped head and plain buffy underparts. Has adapted to the sugar cane belt in the E of the region. **Habitat:** Rank grassland and fields. **Status:** Locally common. **Voice:** Fast, high pitched buzzing. (Rooikeelflap)

15 cm | **Br:** Oct–Apr   J F M A M J J A S O N D

White-winged Widowbird

Could possibly be confused with the Yellow Bishop in br. and non-br. plumages, but this species lacks any yellow on the back or rump and the yellow shoulder patch is bordered by white on the lower edge. Male in non-br. plumage retains the yellow and white shoulder patch. Female lacks the dull yellow rump of female Yellow Bishop. During the non-br. season, flocks in flight are easily recognised by their diagnostic yellow and white shoulder patches. **Habitat:** Found in damp grassy areas and in reed beds. **Status:** Locally common. **Voice:** Zeh-zeh-zeh. (Witvlerkflap)

15–19 cm | **Br:** Dec–May   J F M A M J J A S O N D

Fan-tailed Widowbird

Only two widowbirds in the region have red shoulder patches: this species and the Long-tailed Widowbird. This species is far smaller and the br. male does not have a very long tail. Also, the red shoulder of this species has no broad buff stripe on the lower edge. In non-br. plumage male is easily distinguished by his red shoulder patch, but female lacks any obvious field characters. **Habitat:** Reed beds, rank grassland and stands of sugar cane. **Status:** Common. **Voice:** Various twittering and chirping sounds by male during display. (Kortstertflap)

15–17 cm | **Br:** Oct–Mar   J F M A M J J A S O N D

Long-tailed Widowbird

Unmistakable, with very long tail (40 cm) and bright red shoulder patches bordered with buff. Out of the br. season, the tail is lost and the plumage becomes mottled brown and buff but male retains the red shoulder character. Female is the largest of all female widowbirds, has a rounded wing, floppy flight and shows a dark underwing. When displaying, male flies with the long tail dangling and held spread, and his wings flapping with jerky circular movements. **Habitat**: Open grassland. **Status**: Common. **Voice**: Male gives 'cheet, cheet' and harsher 'zzit, zzit'. (Langstertflap)

♂ 19 cm
♀ 16 cm | Br: Oct–Jun | J F M A M J J A S O N D

Pin-tailed Whydah

Unmistakable pied plumage and very long, black tail (22 cm). Female and non-br. male are a drab mottled brown and buff with dark stripes on the head, but male in this plumage still shows a red bill. In this obscure plumage they can be distinguished from the similarly marked bishops by the dark streaks on the buff head and by the white outer-tail feathers. **Habitat**: Savanna, grassland, scrub, parks and gardens. **Status**: Common. **Voice**: Sharp 'chip-chip-chip', often fluttering in air with tail vertical. (Koningrooibekkie)

12 cm | Br: Aug–May | J F M A M J J A S O N D

Shaft-tailed Whydah

Where the ranges of the Pin-tailed and Shaft-tailed whydahs overlap, it can be difficult to distinguish between them in non-br. plumage. Males in br. plumage are easily differentiated as the Shaft-tailed has warm buff underparts and collar and the tail (22 cm) has diagnostic spatulate tips. The non-br. male and female are slightly paler and have fainter head markings than the similarly plumaged Pin-tailed Whydah. **Habitat**: Grassy areas in acacia savanna. **Status**: Common. **Voice**: High-pitched, squeaky and slurred whistles. (Pylstertrooibekkie)

12 cm | Br: Dec–May | J F M A M J J A S O N D

Long-tailed Paradise Whydah

Br. male unmistakable with black head, orangey-yellow collar and belly and rusty breast band. The tail is exceptionally long (23 cm), stiff, curves downward and tapers gradually to a point. The centre tail feathers are shorter and rounded and are held erect in a display flight. Non-br. male, female and juv. are dowdy brown mottled and streaked with no real distinguishing features. **Habitat**: Woodland and acacia savanna. **Status**: Common, with local movements. **Voice**: Sharp 'chip-chip'. (Gewone paradysvink)

11–13 cm | Br: Jan–Jun | J F M A M J J A S O N D

Purple Indigobird

Resembles Village Indigobird but differs by having white, not red bill, legs and feet. The legs and bill can sometimes appear pinkish. Female, non-br. male and juv. resemble similar sex and age of Village Indigobird but still have whitish, not red bill, legs and feet. When not br., joins mixed flocks of waxbills. **Habitat**: Savanna, especially acacias. **Status**: Common. **Voice**: Mimics purring calls, whistles and trills of its host, Jameson's Firefinch. (Witpootblouvinkie)

11 cm | **Br: Jan–May** | J F M A M J J A S O N D

Village Indigobird

Differs from Purple Indigobird by having red, not white bill and legs. Plumage is wholly jet-black with a slightly paler panel on the folded secondaries. In transitional plumage it has black speckling on the breast and back. Non-br. male, female and juv. are dowdy brown and mottled but still retain the red bill and legs. Birds in the NW of their range have pale pink or whitish bills. **Habitat**: Woodland and savanna. **Status**: Common. **Voice**: Mimics dry, rattling calls and clear, whistled 'wheeet wheeetoo' song of Red-billed Firefinch. (Staalblouvinkie)

11 cm | **Br: Dec–Jun** | J F M A M J J A S O N D

African Firefinch

The grey, not pink crown and nape, and blue, not red bill separate this from the Red-billed Firefinch. Male has a much deeper pinkish-red face and underparts, shading to black on the belly and vent. Female is pinkish-brown below and both sexes have white freckling on sides of breast. Juv. resembles female but is overall duller, being browner below. **Habitat**: Thickets in woodland, savanna and riverine scrub. **Status**: Common. **Voice**: Fast, dry 'trrt-trrt-trrt-trrt' and higher pitched trills; song includes various whistles, including clear 'wink-wink-wink'. (Kaapse vuurvinkie)

10 cm | **Br: Nov–Jun** | J F M A M J J A S O N D

Red-billed Firefinch

The palest pink firefinch and has an obvious pinkish, not blue bill and, at close range, a pale yellow eye-ring. Male has an entirely pinkish-red head and breast. Female is duller with only the rump and upper tail pinkish and is otherwise sandy brown with white spotting on the breast. Juv. resembles female but lacks the white spotting. **Habitat**: Semi-arid woodland, especially near water; also gardens. **Status**: Common. **Voice**: Fairly melodic, slurred 'sweet er-urrrrrr'; sharp, fast 'vut-vut chit-it-errrr'; various dry, chittering or rattling calls. (Rooibekvuurvinkie)

9–10 cm | **Br: Jan–Dec** | J F M A M J J A S O N D

Swee Waxbill **E**

This tiny waxbill is easily recognised by male's grey head, black face, olive back contrasting with bright red rump and black tail. Female is similar to male but lacks the black face and both have black-and-red bills. Juv. resembles female but has all-dark bill. Occurs in small flocks, sometimes in company of Forest Canary and Bronze Mannikin. **Habitat**: Forest edge and densely wooded areas with rank vegetation; also gardens. **Status**: Locally common. **Voice**: 'Swee swee' notes. (Suidelike swie)

9–10 cm | **Br**: Oct–Apr   J F M A M J J A S O N D

Violet-eared Waxbill **NE**

The most colourful waxbill, the male has a cinnamon body, iridescent violet ear patches (diagnostic), a bright blue rump and red eyes and bill. Female and imm. are far paler but still show diagnostic violet ear patches and blue rump. Occurs in pairs or small family parties. Secretive, except when it arrives to drink at waterholes and troughs when it mixes freely with other waxbills and weavers. **Habitat**: Acacia woodland and savanna. **Status**: Common. **Voice**: Dry, buzzy 'tziit'; whistled 'tu-weeoowee'. (Koningblousysie)

15 cm | **Br**: Jul–Aug, Oct–May   J F M A M J J A S O N D

Black-faced Waxbill

Diagnostic features are the greyish head and bold black face patch. Has barred black-and-white wing feathers, dull pinkish underparts and a dark red rump contrasting with an all-black tail. Female and juv. are duller versions of male and have a more patchy black face and a dull reddish-brown rump. **Habitat**: Grassy areas and in thick tangles in dry savanna. **Status**: Common. **Voice**: High-pitched 'chuloweee'. (Swartwangsysie)

12 cm | **Br**: Sep–Mar   J F M A M J J A S O N D

Blue Waxbill

A small, pale brownish waxbill that has a diagnostic powder-blue face and breast. Female is paler than male with less blue on the face and underparts. It feeds on the ground; when disturbed it flies into low areas of bush to hide and gives its soft 'weep-weep' call. Usually occurs in pairs or small flocks and in drier areas frequently visits waterholes or livestock drinking troughs. **Habitat**: Dry woodland, savanna and gardens. **Status**: Common. **Voice**: Soft 'kway-kway-sree-seee-seee-seee'. (Gewone blousysie)

13 cm | **Br**: Aug–Jun   J F M A M J J A S O N D

Common Waxbill

This small waxbill is brownish with a long tail. Best identified by its red bill and eye-stripe, and the small, pink belly patch. Juv. is similar to ad. but is duller and has a black bill. **Habitat**: Favours long grass in damp areas. **Status**: Common resident; gregarious. **Voice**: Call is a nasal 'cher-cher-cher'; 'ping, ping' flight note. (Rooibeksysie)

11–12 cm | **Br: Jan–Dec** | JFMAMJJASOND

Cut-throat Finch

The very obvious pinkish-red band across the throat is diagnostic in the male. General impression is a small finch, heavily barred and mottled with browns and black. Female similar to female Red-headed Finch but is smaller and has a barred, not plain brown head and heavily patterned back. Juv. resembles female but juv. males show a shadow of the red throat band. **Habitat**: Various dry woodlands. **Status**: Locally common. **Voice**: 'Eee-eee-eee' flight call. (Bandkeelvink)

10–11 cm | Br: Jul, Dec–May | JFMAMJJASOND | ♂ ♀

Red-headed Finch   NE

Resembles mostly the Cut-throat Finch but differs by having more uniform upperparts and more heavily scalloped underparts. The red head in the male is diagnostic. Female could be confused with female Cut-throat Finch but has no barring on the head and has a uniform, not barred back. Male in moult can show patchy red head, sometimes with red only on the throat. **Habitat**: Dry grassland, acacia and broad-leaved woodland. **Status**: Common resident and nomad, occasionally erupting outside normal range. **Voice**: Soft 'chuk-chuk'; 'zree, zree' flight call. (Rooikopvink)

13 cm | **Br: Jan–Dec** | JFMAMJJASOND

Scaly-feathered Finch   NE

When in flight this tiny finch appears as a grey blur but, when seen at rest, the contrasting black-and-white malar stripes, freckled black-and-white forehead and white-fringed wing and tail feathers make identification easy. It feeds mostly on the ground and it is not easy to see but when flushed it will settle on bushes in an exposed position. **Habitat**: Dry savanna, bushy desert watercourses and fields. **Status**: Common resident and nomad; often in small groups; joins flocks of other seed-eaters. **Voice**: Soft 'chizz, chizz, chizz' flight call. (Baardmannetjie)

10 cm | **Br: Jan–Dec** | JFMAMJJASOND

Green-winged Pytilia

The red forehead and throat, green breast and back and heavily barred black underparts make this small finch easy to identify. Female lacks the red of male but retains a bright red bill. Juv. resembles female but is more olive above and plain grey below with no barring. **Habitat**: Acacia savanna and dry woodland. **Status**: Common. **Voice**: Dry, chittering song with trilling whistles, often rising and falling in pitch; short 'wick-ick-ick' call. (Gewone melba)

♀

12 cm | Br: Oct–May J F M A M J J A S O N D

African Quail-Finch

The black-and-white face pattern and black-and-white barred breast and flanks are diagnostic. Both sexes have orangey-red bills. Female similar to male but has grey, not black face. Very difficult to see on the ground. Most often seen when flushed and its jerky flight and squeaky call readily identify this species. **Habitat**: Grassland and fields, often near water. **Status**: Common. **Voice**: Distinctive, tinny 'chink-chink' in flight. (Gewone kwartelvinkie)

9 cm | Br: Nov–Jun J F M A M J J A S O N D

Bronze Mannikin

This tiny black-headed bird is easily identified by its brown, black-and-white plumage. The bronze-green shoulder is not easy to see unless the bird is in sunlight, but the barred brown flanks contrast clearly with the white breast. Imm. is completely dun-brown with a small yellow gape: in this plumage imm. would be accompanied by ads. Small groups are often seen huddled side by side on a perch. **Habitat**: Found in grassy areas in woodlands, forest edges and damp regions. **Status**: Abundant. **Voice**: Soft, buzzy 'chizza, chizza'; dry 'krrr krrr'. (Gewone fret)

9 cm | Br: Aug–May J F M A M J J A S O N D

Yellow Canary NE

The 'yellow' canary of the more arid regions. It has a dark form that might be mistaken for a Brimstone or Yellow-fronted canary but it lacks the greenish breast band of the former and the black facial markings of the latter. Much brighter golden-yellow than the pale form Brimstone Canary. Female and imm. differ from female Cape Canary by having whitish, not yellowish-green underparts streaked with brown. **Habitat**: Karoo, coastal scrub and semi-desert. **Status**: Common. **Voice**: Song is similar to that of Yellow-fronted Canary. (Geelkanarie)

♂ ♀

13 cm | Br: Jan–Dec J F M A M J J A S O N D

Brimstone Canary

Largest of the 'yellow' canaries and in all plumages it shows a much heavier, more robust bill. Dark southern birds can be told from the Yellow and Yellow-fronted canaries by their larger size, chunkier bill and the greenish wash across the breast. The more vivid northern birds are distinguished from the Yellow Canary by the more massive bill and by lacking a contrasting yellow rump. **Habitat**: Woodland, mesic thickets and gardens. **Status**: Common; usually in pairs, seldom in flocks. **Voice**: Rich 'zwee zwee' song. (Dikbekkanarie)

13–15 cm | **Br**: May–Mar J F M A M J J A S O N D

Yellow-fronted Canary

Where their ranges overlap, the Yellow-fronted Canary could be confused with male Yellow Canary, but this species has a distinct black line through the eye, a black moustachial stripe and a grey nape, emphasising the yellow around the eye, which the Yellow Canary never shows. It is distinguished from the Brimstone Canary by being smaller and by having a less robust bill. Imm. is a more buffy yellow below. **Habitat**: Open woodland, savanna and gardens. **Status**: Common to abundant. **Voice**: Monotonous 'zeee-zereee, zeee-zereee chereeo'. (Geeloogkanarie)

10–12 cm | **Br**: Sep–Mar J F M A M J J A S O N D

Black-throated Canary

A small, nondescript grey-and-brown canary that has a diagnostic black speckled throat. It also has a bright yellow rump that contrasts with the drab plumage and is conspicuous as the bird takes flight. An active and shy canary, very quick to take flight, it occurs in groups or small flocks. **Habitat**: Acacia savanna, dry woodland and fields in dry regions, often near water. **Status**: Common resident and local nomad; usually in flocks. **Voice**: Prolonged series of wheezy whistles and chirrups. (Bergkanarie)

11 cm | **Br**: Jan–Dec J F M A M J J A S O N D

Cape Canary

The lilting, tinkling call note, unlike that of any other canary, is often the first indication of this species' presence. It differs from the Yellow-fronted Canary by lacking that species' facial markings. Imm. resembles female Yellow Canary but has yellowish-green, not white streaked underparts. **Habitat**: Fynbos, coastal dunes and gardens. **Status**: Common; often in small flocks. **Voice**: Male gives protracted, warbling canary song from prominent perch or in display flight; flight call is distinctive 'su-wi-wi-wi'. (Kaapse kanarie)

11–13 cm | **Br**: Aug–May J F M A M J J A S O N D

White-throated Canary NE

A large, drab canary with a huge bill. The combination of a small white throat patch and greenish-yellow rump is diagnostic. Might be confused with female Yellow Canary but is larger, with a more massive bill and lacks streaking on the breast. Juv. closely resembles ad. but the bill is less well developed. Sexes are similar. **Habitat**: Coastal thicket, Karoo scrub and semi-desert. **Status**: Common. **Voice**: Song is rich, jumbled mix of melodious notes; usual contact call is querulous 'tsuu-eeeee'. (Witkeelkanarie)

15 cm | **Br:** Jan–Dec J F M A M J J A S O N D

Black-headed Canary

A small, nondescript grey and brown canary that has a diagnostic black speckled throat. It also has a bright yellow rump that contrasts with the drab plumage and is conspicuous as the bird takes flight. An active and shy canary, very quick to take flight, it occurs in groups or small flocks. **Habitat**: Acacia savanna, dry woodland and fields in dry regions, often near water. **Status**: Common resident and local nomad; usually in flocks. **Voice**: Prolonged series of wheezy whistles and chirrups. (Swartkopkanarie)

11 cm | **Br:** Jan–Dec J F M A M J J A S O N D

Streaky-headed Seedeater

A fairly large, drab canary with a relatively long, slender bill and a broad, whitish supercilium. Darker above than White-throated Canary, with darker face, more prominent supercilium, and brown, not greenish rump. Juv. more heavily streaked above and below. **Habitat**: Woodland, thickets and dense scrub, often in hilly areas; frequently associated with aloes in drier areas. **Status**: Common. **Voice**: Short, rather deep, melodious song; 'trrreet' contact call. (Streepkopkanarie)

14 cm | **Br:** Sep–Mar J F M A M J J A S O N D

Cape Siskin

A small bird with diagnostic white primaries and tail tips. Female has less extensive white tips to the flight feathers and is less richly coloured than the male. Juv. shows heavy streaking on the head and breast. **Habitat**: Montane fynbos, forest margins, exotic pine plantations. **Status**: Common, localised resident; endemic. **Voice**: Call is 'voyp-veeyr', often given in flight; song is canary-like. (Kaapse Pietjiekanarie)

12 cm | **Br:** Aug–Dec J F M A M J J A S O N D

Golden-breasted Bunting

The black-and-white striped head, chestnut mantle and yellow-orange breast are diagnostic in this bunting. Female and imm. are duller versions of male. Feeds on the ground; when flushed, will fly a short distance, displaying its white outertail, white wing bars and chestnut back. **Habitat**: Woodland and moist savanna. **Status**: Common; usually in pairs. **Voice**: Nasal, buzzy 'zzhrrrr'; song is varied 'weechee, weechee, weechee'. (Rooirugstreepkoppie)

15–16 cm | Br: Oct–Apr

Lark-like Bunting   NE

It is the lack of any definite field characters in this drab and dowdy bird that points to its identification. It might be mistaken for a lark but it exhibits typical bunting behaviour, hopping over stones and grubbing around for seeds on bare ground. It is often flushed from road verges. **Habitat**: Semi-desert plains, Karoo scrub and arid savanna; gathers in large numbers at waterholes to drink. **Status**: Locally abundant nomad; subject to local movements. **Voice**: Song is short series of buzzy notes, accelerating and ending in dry trill; soft 'tuc-tuc' call. (Vaalstreepkoppie)

14 cm | Br: Jan–Dec   J F M A M J J A S O N D

Cape Bunting

The head pattern of this bird resembles that of the Golden-breasted Bunting but is grey and black striped. This, combined with the grey breast and chestnut shoulder, render it easy to identify. Shuffles around on the ground searching for food; when disturbed, it will dash for cover behind a rock or bush. **Habitat**: Rocky hill slopes and scrub. **Status**: Common in S, local and uncommon in N. **Voice**: The call is a nasal, ascending 'zzooo-zeh-zee-zee' and the song, given from a prominent rock, consists of a series of chirping notes. (Rooivlerkstreepkoppie)

16 cm | Br: Jan–Dec   J F M A M J J A S O N D

Cinnamon-breasted Bunting

A dark, richly coloured bunting with bold striping on head. Female and juv. duller, with less bold brown-and-white head markings. Both sexes differ from Cape Bunting by black or greyish, not white throat, and cinnamon, not grey underparts. **Habitat**: Rocky slopes in grassland and open woodland. **Status**: Common. **Voice**: Short, dry, rattling song in S and E; more melodic in W; querulous 'where-wheer' call. (Klipstreepkoppie)

14–15 cm | Br: Oct–Jun   J F M A M J J A S O N D

FURTHER READING

The following books may be of interest to those wishing to learn more about
  birds and bird-watching.

Hardaker, T. & Sinclair, I. 2001. *Birding Map of Southern Africa*. Struik
  Publishers, Cape Town.
Hockey, P., Ryan, P. & Dean, R. 2007. *Roberts Birds of Southern Africa*.
  Black Eagle Publishing, Cape Town.
Newman, K.B. 2002. *Newman's Birds of Southern Africa*. Struik Publishers,
  Cape Town.
Newman, K.B. 2003. *What's that Bird?* Struik Publishers, Cape Town.
Sinclair, I. 1995. *Southern African Birds: A Photographic Guide*. Struik
  Publishers, Cape Town.
Sinclair, I. & Davidson, I. 2006. *Sasol Southern African Birds: A Photographic
  Guide*. Struik Publishers, Cape Town.
Sinclair, I., Hockey, P. & Tarboton, W. 2002. *Sasol Birds of Southern African*.
  Struik Publishers, Cape Town.
Sinclair, I. & Ryan, P. 2003. *Birds of Africa south of the Sahara*. Struik
  Publishers, Cape Town.

Blue Crane

PHOTOGRAPHIC CREDITS

Shaen Adey/Images of Africa: pp 34a, 47c; **Mark Anderson:** pp 25c, 42c, 42d, 69d, 98d1,
107c; **Peter Chadwick:** pp 25b, 49c1; **Peter Craig-Cooper:** pp 46c, 92a, 109d; **Gerald
Cubitt/Images of Africa:** p 81c; **Mike Danzenbaker:** pp 12b, 13d, 14a; **Hannelie de Klerk:**
p 48c; **Roger de la Harpe/Images of Africa:** pp 32b, 43a; **Nigel Dennis:** pp 38c, 134d;
Nigel Dennis/Gallo Images/Afripics: p 21d; **Nigel Dennis/Images of Africa:** pp 15c, 18c,
20b, 21b, 23c1, 23d, 24a, 25d, 26a, 26b, 27a, 28c, 29c1, 29d, 30a, 30b, 30c, 30d, 31b,
32a, 33a, 33b, 33d, 34c, 35b, 35c, 37a, 37b, 37c, 40b, 43d, 44a, 45b, 46a, 47a, 48a, 49b,

49c2, 49d, 50c1, 50d1, 51b, 51c, 52b, 52c, 53a, 53b, 55d, 56b, 57c, 57d, 59b, 60c1, 60d, 62d, 64c, 65b, 66b1, 67a, 68b, 70b, 74b, 75b, 77d, 78c, 79c, 79d1, 80c, 81a, 82c1, 84a, 85a, 86c, 92d, 93a, 93b, 94a, 95c, 97a, 99a1, 110c, 112b, 113b, 116c, 117a, 118a, 118b, 119a, 124d1, 126b, 127d1, 128c1, 130d1, 133a, 133c1, 137a; **Wendy Dennis/Images of Africa:** p 23b; **L N J Du Plessis:** pp 67c, 98a2, 128b1, 130c2, 132b1, 133c2, 134a2; **Derek Engelbrecht:** pp 104a, 106d; **Dick Forsman:** pp 38d, 39b, 54d, 76a; **Albert Froneman:** back cover, pp 16c, 21a2, 22a, 25a, 27c, 28a, 28b, 31c, 34b, 41b, 47b, 52a, 55a, 57a, 61c, 62a, 64d, 69c, 71d, 78a, 81b, 85d, 86d1, 86d2, 87c1, 89a, 90b2, 96d2, 98b, 99b, 99c2, 103b, 105d, 107b, 109a, 111d2, 113c, 114d, 117b, 120a, 120c1, 120d, 121b, 121d1, 121d2, 122a2, 122c2, 123a2, 124c1, 124c2, 125b, 125c1, 125c2, 125d, 126a1, 126a2, 126c1, 127a1, 127a2, 127c2, 129c1, 130a2, 132a2, 132b2, 136c, 137d; **Albert Froneman/Afripics:** pp 16b, 29b, 32c, 46b, 51a, 53d, 56d, 67d, 103a; **Albert Froneman/Images of Africa:** pp 20c, 26d, 36a, 40c, 41d, 43c, 47d, 53c, 55c, 59d1, 59d2, 61a, 61d, 62b, 63a, 64a, 64b, 65a, 65c, 66a, 69b, 70a, 72a, 73d, 74d, 76b, 79a, 84c, 85b, 87a1, 87b1, 88b, 89b, 90a2, 90b1, 90c, 91a2, 91b, 93c, 93d, 94d, 95b, 95d, 96b1, 96d1, 100a, 100b, 100c, 101b, 101c, 102a, 105b, 105c, 106a, 106b, 108c, 108d, 109b, 109c, 111a, 111d1, 112a1, 113d, 115a, 115b, 115d, 116b, 116d, 117d, 118c1, 118c2, 119b, 120c2, 121a, 121c, 122a1, 122c1, 123a1, 123d, 124b1, 127b, 127c1, 128d1, 129b1, 129d1, 129d2, 130a1, 130b1, 130c1, 131c, 131d, 132a1, 132d, 133b, 134a1, 134c, 135a, 135d1, 136a, 137b, 137c; **Gerhard Geldenhuys:** pp 54a, 65d, 71a, 77b2, 77c2, 87a2, 96a1; **Peter Ginn:** p 46d; **John Graham:** pp 13c, 14c, 15b, 16a, 20d2, 21c, 36c, 61b, 102c, 103c, 136d; **Richard Grant:** pp 110d, 122d, 135b; **Nick Greaves:** p 96c2; **Johann Grobbelaar:** pp 40a, 87d2; **Lizet Grobbelaar:** pp 23c2, 50d2; **Clem Haagner:** pp 60a2, 66d; **Martin Hale/VIREO:** p 36d; **Trevor Hardaker:** pp 84b, 98c2; **Martin Harvey/Afripics:** p 45d; **Lex Hes/Afripics:** p 31d, 98d2; **Graham Kearney:** p 66c; **Hanno Langenhoven:** p 70d, 104c; **Mariluo Manning:** p 126d1; **Geoff McIlleron/ Firefly Images:** pp 24d, 41a, 44d, 45a, 54c, 56c, 58a, 63b, 67b, 69a, 70c2, 83d, 84d, 89d, 94c, 101a, 115c, 124a1, 131a; **Rita Meyer:** pp 29c2, 87b2; **Nico Myburgh:** pp 58d, 105a; **Bernie Olbrich/Afripics:** p 45c1; **Deirdre Outram:** p 78d; **Jari Peltomäki:** pp 68d, 76c; **Phil Penlington:** p 114c; **Peter Pickford/Images of Africa:** pp 17c1, 29a, 31a, 33c, 52d, 55b, 57b, 59a, 59c, 75a, 78b; **Darrel Plowes:** p 128d2; **Brian Rode:** p 63c; **Barrie Rose:** pp 21a1, 60a1, 71b, 90a1, 103d, 104b, 106c; **Brendan Ryan:** p 22b; **Peter Ryan:** pp 12a, 17c2, 18a1, 18b1, 24b, 35a, 36b, 38a, 41c, 54b, 72b, 72c, 72d, 73b, 73c, 75d, 76d, 77a, 82b, 82c2, 86a, 90d, 91c, 92b, 95a, 96b2, 96c1, 97b2, 97c, 98a1, 102b, 111c1, 111c2, 112d, 116a, 117c, 119c, 120b, 123c, 124a2, 132c, 133d; **David Shackelford:** p 114b1; **Ian Sinclair:** 12c, 12d, 13a, 13b, 14b, 14d, 15a, 16d, 17a1, 17a2, 17b, 17d, 18a2, 18b2, 19a, 19b, 19c, 19d, 20a, 20d1, 23a, 24c, 27b, 27d, 28d, 32d, 34d, 35d, 38b, 39a, 39c, 40d, 42b, 50a1, 50a2, 50b1, 50b2, 50c2, 56a, 60b2, 60c2, 66b2, 70c1, 73a, 74c, 79d2, 81d, 88d, 89c, 92c, 97b1, 107a, 108b, 112c, 113a, 126c2, 127d2, 128a, 129a2, 135c, 135d2; **Philip Stapelberg:** pp 110b, 122b2; **J G Swanepoel:** pp 80a, 114b2; **Warwick Tarboton:** pp 15d, 22c, 26c, 42a, 43b, 44c, 45c2, 48d, 49a, 58b, 58c, 71c, 75c, 83a, 85c, 91a1, 94b, 96a2, 99a2, 99c1, 100d, 101d, 102d, 107d, 108a, 111b, 112a2, 119d, 123b2, 124b2, 124d2, 126d2, 128b2, 128c2, 129c2, 130b2, 130d2, 134b, 136b; **Ray Tipper:** pp 74a, 87c2, 98c1, 110a; **Ann & Steve Toon:** pp 39d, 51d, 80b, 80d; **Guy Upfold:** front cover, pp 86b, 122b1, 123b1; **Rudi van Aarde:** pp 22d, 48b; **Philip van den Berg:** pp 88c, 97d, 114a; **D J van Niekerk:** pp 44b, 62c, 63d, 131b; **Chris van Rooyen:** pp 68a, 68c2, 77c1, 79b, 82d, 83b, 83c, 87d1, 91d, 99d, 118d, 125a, 129a1, 129b2; **Daniel Voges:** p 77b1; **Alan Weaving:** pp 18d, 37d, 60b1; **Robin Weeks:** pp 82a, 104d; **Mike Yudaken:** p 88a

INDEX

A
Albatross
Atlantic Yellow-nosed **12**
Black-browed **12**
Apalis
Bar-throated **106**
Yellow-breasted **105**
Avocet
Pied **33**
B
Babbler
Arrow-marked **93**
Southern Pied **93**
Barbet
Acacia Pied **85**
Black-collared **84**
Crested **85**
White-eared **84**
Bateleur 52
Batis
Cape **111**
Chinspot **112**
Pririt **111**
Bee-eater
Blue-cheeked **79**
European **79**
Little **80**
Southern Carmine **79**
Swallow-tailed **80**
White-fronted **79**
Bishop
Southern Red **128**
Yellow **129**
Yellow-crowned **128**
Bokmakierie 116
Boubou
Southern **115**
Tropical **115**
Brownbul
Terrestrial **94**
Brubru 117
Buffalo Weaver
Red-billed **125**
Bulbul
African Red-eyed **94**
Cape **93**
Dark-capped **94**

Bunting
Cape **137**
Cinnamon-breasted **137**
Golden-breasted **137**
Lark-like **137**
Bushshrike
Grey-headed **116**
Orange-breasted **116**
Bustard
Black-bellied **48**
Denham's **48**
Kori **48**
Buttonquail
Common **46**
Buzzard
Augur **54**
Jackal **55**
Lizard **57**
Steppe **55**
C
Camaroptera
Green-backed **104**
Grey-backed **104**
Canary
Black-headed **136**
Black-throated **135**
Brimstone **135**
Cape **135**
White-throated **136**
Yellow **134**
Yellow-fronted **135**
Chat
Ant-eating **99**
Buff-streaked **99**
Familiar **97**
Karoo **97**
Mocking Cliff **99**
Sickle-winged **97**
Tractrac **97**
Cisticola
Desert **106**
Grey-backed **107**
Levaillant's **107**
Rattling **107**
Red-faced **107**
Zitting **106**
Cliff-Swallow

South African **74**
Coot
Red-knobbed **25**
Cormorant
Bank **15**
Cape **15**
Crowned **15**
Reed **16**
White-breasted **15**
Coucal
Burchell's **70**
Senegal **71**
White-browed **71**
Courser
Bronze-winged **42**
Burchell's **42**
Double-banded **42**
Temminck's **42**
Crake
Black **26**
Crane
Blue **47**
Grey Crowned **47**
Crombec
Long-billed **105**
Crow
Cape **92**
House **92**
Pied **92**
Cuckoo
African **69**
Black **69**
Common **68**
Dideric **70**
Great Spotted **70**
Jacobin **69**
Klaas's **70**
Red-chested **69**
Cuckooshrike
Black **91**
Curlew
Eurasian **39**
D
Darter
African **16**
Dove
Cape Turtle **65**

Emerald-spotted Wood 65
Laughing 65
Namaqua 66
Red-eyed 65
Rock 64
Tambourine 66
Drongo
Fork-tailed 90
Duck
African Black 24
Fulvous Whistling 23
Knob-billed 22
Maccoa 25
White-backed 25
White-faced Whistling 22
Yellow-billed 23
E
Eagle
Booted 54
Crowned 53
Long-crested 54
Tawny 53
Verreaux's 53
Wahlberg's 54
Eagle-Owl
Spotted 61
Verreaux's 61
Egret
Great White 27
Little 27
Western Cattle 27
Yellow-billed 27
Eremomela
Yellow-bellied 102
F
Falcon
Amur 59
Lanner 59
Peregrine 59
Pygmy 57
Red-footed 60
Finch
Cut-throat 133
Red-headed 133
Scaly-feathered 133
Firefinch
African 131
Red-billed 131
Fiscal

Common 114
Fish Eagle
African 52
Flamingo
Greater 33
Lesser 33
Flycatcher
African Dusky 109
African Paradise 111
Ashy 109
Chat 110
Fairy 105
Fiscal 110
Marico 110
Pale 110
Southern Black 109
Spotted 109
Francolin
Coqui 45
Crested 45
Grey-winged 44
Orange River 44
Red-winged 44
Shelley's 45
G
Gannet
Cape 18
Go-Away-Bird
Grey 68
Godwit
Bar-tailed 38
Goose
Egyptian 22
Spur-winged 21
Goshawk
African 59
Dark Chanting 56
Gabar 57
Pale Chanting 56
Grassbird
Cape 104
Grebe
Black-necked 21
Great Crested 21
Little 21
Greenbul
Sombre 94
Yellow-bellied 95
Greenshank

Common 38
Ground-Hornbill
Southern 81
Guineafowl
Crested 46
Helmeted 45
Gull
Grey-headed 17
Hartlaub's 17
Kelp 17
Sabine's 17
H
Hamerkop 40
Harrier
Black 56
Harrier-Hawk
African 55
Helmetshrike
White-crested 117
Heron
Black 29
Black-crowned Night 29
Black-headed 28
Goliath 28
Green-backed 29
Grey 28
Purple 28
Squacco 29
Honeyguide
Greater 84
Lesser 84
Hoopoe
African 83
Hornbill
African Grey 82
Crowned 82
Monteiro's 82
Southern 81
Southern Red-billed 83
Southern Yellow-billed 82
Trumpeter 81
I
Ibis
African Sacred 32
Glossy 32
Hadeda 32
Southern Bald 32
Indigobird
Purple 131

Village **131**

J

Jacana
African **26**

K

Kestrel
Greater **60**
Lesser **60**
Rock **60**

Kingfisher
African Pygmy **78**
Brown-hooded **78**
Giant **77**
Malachite **77**
Pied **77**
Striped **78**
Woodland **78**

Kite
Black-shouldered **57**
Yellow-billed **56**

Knot
Red **34**

Korhaan
Blue **49**
Karoo **48**
Northern Black **49**
Red-crested **49**
Southern Black **49**

L

Lapwing
African Wattled **41**
Blacksmith **41**
Black-winged **40**
Crowned **40**
Senegal **41**
White-crowned **41**

Lark
Cape Long-billed **89**
Eastern Long-billed **89**
Fawn-coloured **88**
Flappet **88**
Large-billed **88**
Red-capped **89**
Rufous-naped **89**
Sabota **88**
Spike-heeled **90**

Longclaw
Cape **113**
Yellow-throated **113**

Lovebird
Rosy-faced **67**

M

Mannikin
Bronze **134**

Marsh-Harrier
African **55**

Martin
Banded **76**
Brown-throated **76**
Common House **76**
Rock **77**
Sand **76**

Masked Weaver
Lesser **127**
Southern **126**

Moorhen
Common **26**

Mousebird
Red-faced **71**
Speckled **71**
White-backed **72**

Myna
Common **120**

N

Neddicky 106

Nightjar
Fiery-necked **63**
Freckled **63**
Rufous-cheeked **63**

O

Olive-Pigeon
African **64**

Openbill
African **31**

Oriole
Blackheaded **93**

Ostrich
Common **47**

Owl
Barn **61**
Southern White-faced **62**
Western Marsh **62**

Owlet
African Barred **62**
Pearl-spotted **62**

Oxpecker
Red-billed **121**

Oystercatcher

African (Black) **34**

P

Palm Swift
African **73**

Parrot
Brown-headed **67**
Cape **66**
Grey-headed **66**
Meyer's **67**

Pelican
Great White **16**
Pink-backed **16**

Penduline-Tit
Cape **102**
Grey **102**

Penguin
African **18**

Petrel
Pintado **14**
Southern Giant **12**
White-chinned **12**

Petronia
Yellow-throated **125**

Pigeon
African Green **64**
Speckled **64**

Pipit
African **113**
Long-billed **112**

Plover
Chestnut-banded **35**
Common Ringed **35**
Grey **38**
Kittlitz's **35**
Three-banded **35**
White-fronted **36**

Pochard
Southern **23**

Prinia
Black-chested **108**
Karoo **108**
Tawny-flanked **108**

Prion
Antarctic **14**

Puffback
Black-backed **117**

Pygmy Goose
African **23**

Pytilia

Green-winged **134**

Q

Quail
Common **46**
Harlequin **46**

Quail-Finch
African **134**

Quelea
Red-billed **128**

R

Raven
White-necked **92**

Reed-Warbler
African **103**
Great **103**

Robin-Chat
Cape **100**
Chorister **99**
Red-capped **100**
White-browed **100**
White-throated **100**

Rock-jumper
Cape **98**
Drakensberg **98**

Rock-Thrush
Cape **96**
Sentinel **96**
Short-toed **96**

Roller
Broad-billed **81**
European **80**
Lilac-breasted **80**
Purple **81**

Ruff 34

Rush-Warbler
Little **103**

S

Sanderling 36

Sandgrouse
Burchell's **50**
Double-banded **50**
Namaqua **50**
Yellow-throated **50**

Sandpiper
Common **37**
Curlew **37**
Marsh **38**
Terek **37**
Wood **37**

Sand-Plover
Greater **36**

Saw-wing
Black **75**

Scimitarbill
Common **83**

Scops-Owl
African **63**

Scrubrobin
Bearded **101**
Kalahari **101**
Karoo **101**
White-browed **101**

Secretarybird 47

Seedeater
Streaky-headed **136**

Shearwater
Cory's **13**
Great **13**
Sooty **13**

Shelduck
South African **22**

Shikra 58

Shoveler
Cape **24**

Shrike
Crimson-breasted **113**
Lesser Grey **114**
Magpie **114**
Red-backed **114**
Southern White-
crowned **117**

Siskin
Cape **136**

Skua
Subantarctic **13**

Snake Eagle
Black-chested **53**
Brown **52**

Snipe
African **40**

Sparrow
Cape **124**
House **124**
Southern Grey-
headed **125**

Sparrowhawk
Black **58**
Little **58**

Rufous-chested **58**

Sparrow-Lark
Chestnut-backed **90**
Grey-backed **90**

Sparrow-Weaver
White browed **125**

Spoonbill
African **31**

Spurfowl
Cape **43**
Natal **44**
Red-billed **43**
Red-necked **43**
Swainson's **43**

Starling
Black-bellied **118**
Burchell's **119**
Cape Glossy **118**
Common **120**
Greater Blue-eared **118**
Meve's **119**
Pale-winged **119**
Pied **120**
Red-winged **119**
Violet backed **118**
Wattled **120**

Stilt
Black-winged **33**

Stint
Little **36**

Stonechat
African **96**

Stork
Abdim's **30**
Marabou **30**
Saddle-billed **31**
White **30**
Woolly-necked **31**
Yellow-billed **30**

Storm-Petrel
European **14**
Wilson's **14**

Sugarbird
Cape **121**
Gurney's **121**

Sunbird
Amethyst **122**
Collared **123**
Dusky **123**

Greater Double-collared 123
Malachite 121
Marico 124
Olive 122
Orange-breasted 122
Scarlet-chested 122
Southern Double-
collared 124
White-bellied 123
Swallow
Barn 74
Greater Striped 74
Lesser Striped 74
Pearl-breasted 75
Red-breasted 73
White-throated 75
Wire-tailed 75
Swamphen
African 26
Swampwarbler
Lesser 103
Swift
African Black 72
Alpine 72
Common 72
Little 73
White-rumped 73
T
Tchagra
Black-crowned 115
Brown-crowned 115
Southern 116
Teal
Cape 24
Hottentot 25
Red-billed 24
Tern
Antarctic 19
Arctic 19
Caspian 18
Common 19
Damara 20
Lesser Crested 18

Little 20
Swift 19
Whiskered 20
White-winged 20
Thick-knee
Spotted 39
Water 39
Thrush
Groundscraper 95
Kurrichane 95
Olive 95
Tinkerbird
Red-fronted 86
Yellow-fronted 85
Yellow-rumped 85
Tit
Ashy 91
Grey 91
Southern Black 91
Tit-Babbler
Chestnut-vented 105
Trogon
Narina 68
Turaco
Knysna 67
Purple-crested 68
Turnstone
Ruddy 34
V
Vulture
Bearded 51
Cape 51
Lappet-faced 51
White-backed 52
White-headed 51
W
Wagtail
African Pied 112
Cape 112
Warbler
Rufous-eared 108
Sedge 104
Willow 102

Waxbill
Black-faced 132
Blue 132
Common 133
Swee 132
Violet-eared 132
Weaver
Cape 127
Red-headed 127
Sociable 126
Spectacled 127
Thick-billed 126
Village 126
Yellow 128
Wheatear
Capped 98
Mountain 98
Whimbrel
Common 39
White-eye
Cape 111
Whydah
Long-tailed Paradise 130
Pin-tailed 130
Shaft-tailed 130
Widowbird
Fan-tailed 129
Long-tailed 130
Red-collared 129
White-winged 129
Wood-Hoopoe
Green 83
Wood-Owl
African 61
Woodpecker
Bearded 87
Bennett's 87
Cardinal 87
Golden-tailed 87
Ground 86
Olive 86
Wryneck
Red-throated 86